Vegetable Growing
Month by Month

Roy Genders

WARD LOCK LIMITED · LONDON

Acknowledgements

The publishers gratefully acknowledge the
Harry Smith Horticultural Photographic
Collection for permission to reproduce the
colour photographs shown on the cover and on
pp. 17, 18, 35, 36, 53, 54, 71 and 72.

First published in Great Britain in 1979
by Ward Lock Limited, 116 Baker Street,
London W1M 2BB, Pentos company.

Text filmset in V-I-P Times

Printed and bound in Great Britain by
Cox & Wyman Ltd, London,
Fakenham and Reading

British Library Cataloguing in Publication Data

Genders, Roy
    Vegetable growing month by month. –
    (Concorde books).
    1. Vegetable gardening
    I. Title   II. Series
    635   SB322

ISBN 0–7063–5506–7
ISBN 0–7063–5507–5   Pbk

Vegetable Growing Month by Month

Contents

PUBLISHER'S NOTE

Readers are requested to note that in the vast majority of cases the measurements in this book are cited in both metric and Imperial quantities. In a few instances, owing to space limitations, only the metric quantity has been cited.

Preface

There are now more and more people growing their own vegetables, not only because they are expensive to buy but because fresh vegetables straight from the garden are always preferable to those from packets and tins. Also, the rise in the number of deep freeze units in Britain has given vegetable growing an additional value, for all those crops surplus to the household's immediate requirements can now be frozen to provide fresh vegetables all the year round. Not only is there no waste but it is most useful to have home grown vegetables available at a time when there is always a shortage in the shops and when they are most expensive. They are also available from the freezer exactly when required, there is no need to go out in poor weather looking for them. But whilst amateur gardeners find little difficulty in the growing of vegetables, I am often asked exactly when to sow a certain crop and when it should be used either fresh or to place in the freezer. Gardeners are familiar with each of the different crops but find difficulty in knowing which will mature early or late, so extending the season and this is the way to crop the garden to best advantage.

So this book has been written for those who are new to vegetable growing and shows exactly what crops should be sown each month of the year and when they are ready to use. It is hoped that much of the guesswork of vegetable growing will be eliminated and the result will be more and better crops.

1 January

GENERAL CULTIVATIONS

The beginning of a new year is perhaps the best time to prepare the ground for most food crops but only if the soil is not water-logged or frost-bound. Preparation of the ground may be done at any time between the end of October until mid-March, whenever the soil is in a friable condition. There is nothing more harmful to soil than to tread it when it sticks to the boots, making it so compact that it will set like concrete when the weather becomes dry and thus deprive the growing plants with the necessary oxygen and moisture. Conditioning of the soil will continue all the year, whenever a crop is cleared and before another is sown or planted, but when this takes place the preparation will not be done so well as when the ground is made ready in winter for the year's cropping ahead. The better the soil is prepared, the better will be the crops; what is put into the ground by way of hard work and as humus and fertilizers will be rewarded by high yields and the quality of the vegetables.

TOOLS REQUIRED

First, purchase a good spade and a garden fork, preferably of stainless steel so that they may be kept clean and wipe them with an oily rag after use. In this way the soil will not cling to them, neither will they become rusted. This will make for easier working. A light barrow will be useful for moving rubbish and weeds to the compost heap and organic manure to the land. A hose pipe or sprinkler will be necessary, for vegetables require plenty of water if they are to be tender and succulent and during dry weather, artificial watering will be essential. A supply of water may be taken from the kitchen or from an outside tap whilst for those with an allotment away from a mains supply, rain water may be collected in a galvanized tank or barrel from the roof of a shed or small greenhouse. But there is little chance of growing good vegetable crops unless a water supply is available. An efficient watering can will also be a necessity.

Amongst other tools needed will be a rake; a hoe; and a trowel, and a garden line will be useful when planting and to obtain the correct spacing of the rows. This is important for while the best use must be made of the ground which means that the plants should not be spaced too far apart, too close planting will cause the plants to be deprived of moisture, sunlight and food and they will either grow stunted or weak and spindly.

A rake will be needed to bring the soil of a prepared seed bed to a fine tilth whilst the rows in which to sow the seeds are made with the back of the rake using a garden line to ensure straightness.

A hoe of the Dutch type or what is known as a scuffle hoe will be necessary to break up the soil between the plants. This is best done during dry weather when the sun or wind will kill the weeds and by stirring the soil, moisture is allowed to reach down to the roots of the plants when it rains or when the plants are watered. It will also prevent the surface from 'panning', when the soil sets hard and prevents air and moisture reaching the roots.

A few glass or plastic cloches will be an advantage and will mean that earlier crops can be grown by protecting the plants from cold winds and by harbouring the maximum of the winter and early spring sunshine.

Glass cloches are of barn- or tent-type, the panes being held together by galvanized wires which are rust-proof. Barn cloches are 60cm (24in) long and 58cm (23in) wide when made up, whilst they are 30cm (12in) at the highest point. This width allows a double or treble row of seedlings or of French beans or lettuce plants to be set out beneath them. The tent cloche is only 38cm (15in) wide and 25cm (10in) high and is suitable for covering a single row of plants. Marrows,

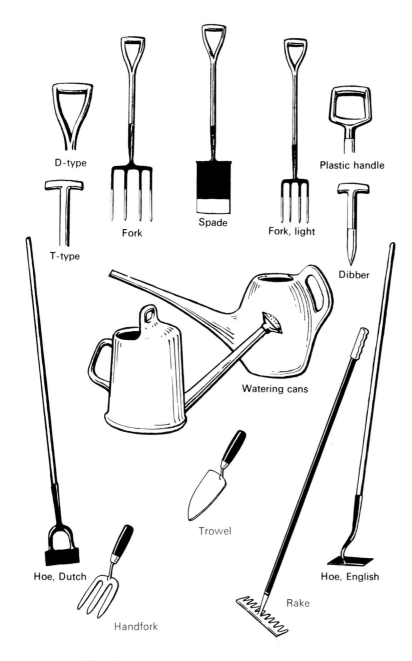

D-type

Fork

Spade

Fork, light

Plastic handle

T-type

Dibber

Watering cans

Trowel

Hoe, Dutch

Handfork

Rake

Hoe, English

Basic tools. The diagram shows most of the basic tools needed

cucumbers and bush tomatoes may be grown under barn cloches, from planting to cropping and they can then be used to cover winter lettuce or cauliflowers, or autumn-fruiting strawberries, thus keeping the cloches employed all the year round. They may also be used to raise early turnips, carrots and radishes, the method being to remove soil to the width of the cloches and to a depth of 15–20cm (6–8in) and to replace with 15cm (6in) of hot stable manure. This is trodden down to enable it to retain its heat and 8cm (3in) of soil is placed over the top. Into this the seeds are sown in rows 10cm (4in) apart. To exclude draughts, end pieces are obtainable to cover each end of the row.

Another form of cloche is made with sheets of Claritex, a virtually unbreakable and rigid perspex which is frost-proof and will make a cloche of sufficient width to take three rows of lettuce. The cloche is held secure by galvanized steel wire hoops. Using steel hoops for its shape, an inexpensive and long tunnel cloche may be made up from ICI's PVC sheeting which is durable yet light to handle and can easily be stored after use.

A supply of 180–240cm (6–8ft) canes or builder's laths will be useful for runner beans or they may be grown up wire or plastic netting, whilst some 120cm (4ft) canes will be needed for outdoor tomatoes unless it is intended to grow the dwarf kinds like 'Puck' and 'The Amateur' which need no staking.

Where using a warm frame in which to raise tomatoes, marrows and aubergines, a supply of Vacapot trays or Jiffypots or Root-o-Pots which are cubes made of peat fortified with plant foods are rewarding. Vacapots are thin-walled containers divided into 24 units, each container being a 5cm (2in) cube. The cubes are filled with sowing mix and into each, a single seedling is planted as soon as it is large enough to handle. When planting on, the seedling is moved with the soil ball intact. If Jiffypots or Root-o-Pots are used, the young plants are potted on or set out with the cubes intact.

DRAINING AND PREPARING THE SOIL

If the soil is of a heavy clay nature or has become compact through not being worked for some time, drainage materials should be incorporated. These may take the form of crushed

Plain digging

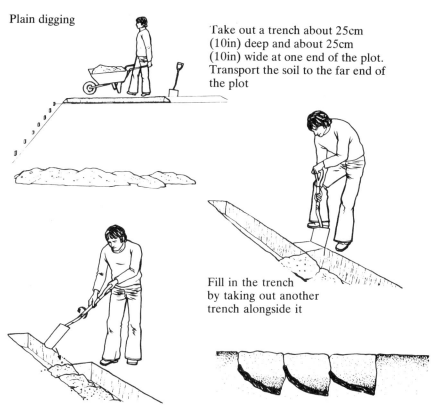

Take out a trench about 25cm (10in) deep and about 25cm (10in) wide at one end of the plot. Transport the soil to the far end of the plot

Fill in the trench by taking out another trench alongside it

Repeat the process, filling in the final trench with the soil taken from the first one. Manure or compost can be placed at the bottom of each trench as you go

Always face the trench and turn the soil forward and over so that any weeds are buried at the bottom of the first trench

brick from a building site or mortar, gravel or shingle, whilst boiler ash and clearings from ditches are also suitable. As the ground is dug over the drainage materials are added to the lower or second 'spit' or spade depth and this will allow surplus winter moisture to drain away. This will prevent the soil becoming sour whilst if excess winter moisture remains about the roots of the plants, it may cause them to decay as with broccoli, Brussels sprouts and cabbages which may occupy the ground throughout the winter months.

13

Every type of soil will need lime, not only to correct the soil's acidity which in town gardens is often high, but also because lime has the ability to release the various plant foods pent up in the soil so that where absent, manures and fertilizers are unable to play their part in producing top quality crops. In other words, they are mostly wasted. Again, lime is able to improve the quality of a heavy soil by breaking up the clay particles. For this purpose try to get caustic or unhydrated lime from a builders' merchant and apply it to the soil when it is in a friable condition. When in contact with moisture in the ground, an explosive action takes place causing the soil particles to disintegrate with the lime.

When liming ordinary soil or that of a town garden, use hydrated lime and merely scatter it over the surface before digging commences. About 3·5kg (7lb) of lime will be required for every 30sq m (100sq ft) of ground and it should be applied in winter, between November and March.

It is possible to grow good vegetables without the use of organic manures (using peat or decayed leaves for humus) or without the use of artificial (chemical) fertilizers but a combination of both will give the best results. Artificial fertilizers are more effective when the land is in good 'heart', containing plenty of organic matter such as farmyard manure, composted straw, bark fibre, leaf mould or peat. No soil will grow good crops without plenty of humus and the form of humus to be used should be that which is most easily obtained. Humus will open up a heavy soil and enable a light, sandy soil to retain summer moisture. It will also add depth to a thin, calcareous soil.

To grow vegetables well, a balanced diet is necessary; farmyard manure and pig and poultry manure contain nitrogen, potash and phosphates, and where obtainable, should be used. They also provide humus. Old mushroom bed compost contains a number of plant foods whilst bone meal is rich in phosphates and nitrogen. Wood and bonfire ash contain potash but should be stored under cover so that the rains cannot wash away the potash. Hop manure, obtainable as 'used hops' from a brewery is another source of humus and provides nitrogen and phosphates, and 'shoddy', which is wool and cotton waste and is readily obtainable in northern

England, has a useful nitrogen content. Each of these organic fertilizers releases its food content slowly, throughout the life of the crop.

Where these manures are obtainable only in limited supply, it will be necessary to use artificial or inorganic manures to augment them. These are usually obtained as nitrate of soda which has a high nitrogen content; likewise sulphate of ammonia. Plants require nitrogen to make leaf and size: without it they grow stunted and hard. They need potash to survive a severe winter and to mature correctly. This is given as sulphate of potash. Phosphates are needed to stimulate root action and are given as superphosphate of lime. Potash will also improve the flavour of vegetables.

DOUBLE DIGGING

To clean and prepare neglected ground, double digging is done. This means preparing the ground to a depth of two 'spits' or spades deep. Drainage materials and humus are placed in the bottom of the trench and into the top 'spit', manures are incorporated and at the same time all perennial weeds should be taken out. The work is best done in small sections and should be completed by early March to allow the

Double digging

Use a garden line to divide the plot lengthwise. Drive pegs in at 60cm (2ft) intervals. Take out a trench 60cm (2ft) wide and the depth of a spade deep. Move the soil as shown

Fork over the bottom of the trench

15

 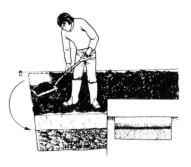

Take out a second 60cm (2ft) trench and use the soil to fill in the first one. Note how the soil is dug and where each spadeful is placed

Manure can be spread over the bottom of the trench after forking or it can be spread over the surface to be dug

ground a week or so to consolidate itself before planting begins. The ground must be limed, for where lime is absent, the soil is unable to release its fertilizer content to the full extent. Hydrated lime is obtained from a builders' merchant and is spread over the ground as the work proceeds.

Land which has been neglected for some years should also be treated for wireworm. Gamma-BHC powder is effective but must not be used on ground that is to be planted with potatoes the same year.

THE USE OF A FRAME

For garden operations to begin early in the new year so that the most may be made of the vegetable garden, a cold frame may be obtained or one may be simply constructed from an old window frame covered with plastic sheeting. The frame light, or lid, should rest on a base made from old railway sleepers, breeze blocks, or boarding held in place by stakes driven well into the ground. There should be 30–38cm (12–15in) of clearance room from soil level to the top of the frame for the plants to grow.

A heated frame will give additional scope for raising early crops. Where an electric supply is available, air warming cables can be fitted to the sides of a frame by means of clips and to warm a frame 150×120cm (5×4ft), a 300 watt air warming cable will be needed. It will cost only a few pence

Brussels sprouts; note that about 60cm (2ft) is left between each plant

Carrot, variety 'Redcored Chantenay'

daily to run during the winter months and will enable a crop of winter lettuce to be enjoyed, followed by early carrots and turnips.

Where the electric supply is not available, a hot bed may be prepared. This is done by removing soil to the depth of about 23cm (9in) (the depth of a spade) and replacing it with a quantity of prepared stable manure, or straw which has been made wet and treated with an activator. When dark brown in colour it is placed in the frame and trodden well down to retain its heat. Over the top place 8cm (3in) of fresh loam and seeds can be sown directly into this or in small pots which are pressed into the soil. The heat generated by the hot bed ensures early crops. The frame light is kept in place so that heat is not lost and if the weather is unduly cold, cover the light at night with sacking held in place with bricks. It will be an advantage to have both a warm and a cold frame.

CROPS TO SOW OUTDOORS IN JANUARY
Beans, broad Before the month's end, sow outdoors the 'Longpod' varieties; the less hardy 'Windsors' should not be sown until March. In a sheltered garden south of the Trent, sowings may be made in October and again in January and may be left unprotected through winter. North of the Trent, cover with cloches in winter or delay sowing until March.

To sow, take out a trench 23–25cm (9–10in) wide and 15cm (6in) deep and place in it some decayed manure or garden compost, replacing 8cm (3in) of soil afterwards. Sow the seed in a double row made 15cm (6in) apart, allowing 10cm (4in) between the seeds in the rows. Sow about 5cm (2in) deep with a trowel. Autumn and winter sown beans are rarely troubled by black fly. Reliable 'Longpods' are 'Promotion', which forms long straight pods 20–25cm (8–10in) long; and 'Aquadulce' which bears 8 or 9 beans to a pod. The pods are 30–38cm (12–15in) long. It crops early, is hardy and is a prolific cropper.

Remove cloches from winter-covered plants about mid-March and use the cloches to cover newly planted lettuce or cauliflowers.

Broad beans may also be sown in deep boxes in a cold frame at this time so that they can be transplanted to the open

19

ground early in March. If cold winds persist at the time, cover with cloches until early April.

VEGETABLES TO HARVEST IN JANUARY

Brussels sprouts   In January, those sprouts such as 'Peer Gynt' which come early in winter may be past their best but those later to mature, such as 'Roodnerf', 'Sigmund', and 'Citadel' will be at top quality and will yield until the end of March, long after the early kinds have finished. So always sow early and late varieties to have sprouts from September until Easter.

Cabbage (winter) and Savoy   Those cabbages and savoys with crinkled leaves, by which the heavy winter rains can drain away quickly, will now be ready and will be at their best after frost. One is 'Savoy King' which makes a huge tight head with few outer leaves and stands the severest weather. 'January King' is blue in colour which signifies its hardiness and the heads are crisp and crunchy. 'Christmas Drumhead' makes a smaller head but is equally hardy and is suitable for a small garden. 'Jupiter' matures earlier in winter; if cut and placed in a shed in December, will remain fresh until February.

Celeriac   Celeriac 'Globus' may be left in the ground and used when required though in cold, exposed northern gardens, it will be better to lift the roots mid-December before hard frosts make this difficult. Remove the leaves and store the roots in sand to use as required.

Celery   Celery which needs blanching will be available now. Best for a small garden is 'New Dwarf White' which grows to only half the height of others but makes a thick solid heart, whilst 'Suttons Giant Red' is reliable for later. Celery improves with frost and can be lifted from November until March except when the ground is frozen hard.

Kale   Curly kale will also be available at this time and the best variety is 'Pentland Brigg'. Extremely hardy, it crops right through winter until Easter and is crisp and tender. The older 'Dwarf Green Curled' is also hardy.

20

Mustard and cress Sow mustard, and rape seed which has a better flavour than cress, in boxes or pans in the kitchen window, or in a frame at fortnightly intervals throughout winter and enjoy it on scrambled eggs and in sandwiches. It may be grown without soil, scattering the seed thickly on a piece of flannel and keeping it moist. It will be ready to use within two to three weeks.

Onions Onions lifted in late October and strung up in a frost-free place can be used as required but in mild parts, spring or salad onions sown in the open in early autumn may be ready to begin using before the end of January.

Potatoes Maincrop potatoes and sweet potatoes will be available at this time. Sweet potatoes with their dahlia-like roots will have been stored in boxes of sand. Maincrop potatoes will be stored in a clamp in a shed or garage or in boxes or sacks for winter use. Potatoes must be kept away from frost.

Spinach Winter spinach may be gathered fresh at this time. It is rich in iron and calcium and is a health-giving addition to the diet at this time. Available now will be 'Perpetual Spinach' and 'Longstanding Prickly', both of which will continue to make leaf during all but the severest weather.

Root crops In January, maincrop turnips and swedes, also parsnips are available, having been lifted in December and after removing the tops, stored in boxes of sand or peat in a cellar or shed. In a mild winter climate, these roots may be left in the ground and lifted as required when the flavour and eating qualities will be improved by frost.

Carrots are not improved by frost and are best lifted in November and stored in a frost-free room. Use also at this time in salads, the winter radish 'China Rose' which will have been lifted in November and stored in sand.

2 February

GENERAL CULTIVATIONS

Often the coldest month of winter, the frames should be kept closed on all but the sunniest days when ventilation is necessary, though they should be closed by late afternoon to harbour the last hours of warm sunshine for night protection. Cover frame lights with sacking or bracken if available, whenever there is the likelihood of a hard frost at night.

Do not overwater seedlings which will be through before the month's end from sowings made in January. Do any watering at mid-day to enable surplus moisture to evaporate before nightfall.

By the month's end, the surface of the soil will have become hardened after winter rains and February sunshine, and the hoe should be used between rows of vegetables which have been standing through winter – but not when the ground is sticky after frost or rain.

After stirring the surface, give spring cabbage and sprouting broccoli a boost by a 30g/sq m (1oz/sq yd) dressing of sulphate of ammonia. This will stimulate the plants into growth assisted by the warmer weather and they will soon lose their starved 'blue' look.

If it was not done earlier, now is the time to take out a trench for runner beans. This should be 38cm (15in) deep. Heap the soil on one side and fill the trench with anything that will be converted into moisture-retaining humus, for runner beans need ample supplies of moisture at the roots or they will drop their flowers before they set. Garden compost, old newspapers, tea leaves and potato peelings, all kinds of

22

Sowing seeds in a seedbox

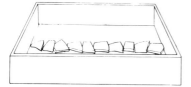

Put a line of crocks along the bottom of the box (unless you are using a plastic box)

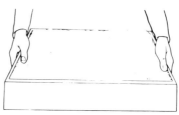

Slightly overfill the box with a seed growing mix and then gently tap it to settle the mix

Remove excess mix with a straight edge

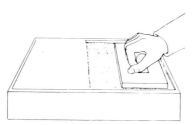

Firm gently with a rectangular template

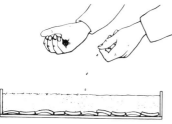

Sow the seeds thinly. Large seeds can be sown individually to prevent the necessity of pricking them out later

Cover the seed with sieved growing mix

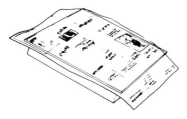

Place a newspaper and a sheet of glass over the seedbox. Both should be removed as soon as the seeds germinate

organic waste will be suitable, together with a small amount of farmyard manure or used hops. After putting an 8cm (3in) layer in the bottom of the trench, add 5cm (2in) of soil and build up the trench in sandwich fashion during February and March.

VEGETABLES TO PLANT OR SOW OUTDOORS IN FEBRUARY

Artichoke, Jerusalem   This is a tuber, like the potato, and grows under the soil. The tubers are used through autumn and winter and are nourishing, with a unique flavour.

As the tubers begin to make growth early, plant late in February, or early March in the north. A light, sandy soil suits them best though humus is necessary to retain summer moisture. Plant walnut-size tubers 13cm (5in) deep and 30cm (12in) apart but as they will grow tall, allow twice that distance between the rows. Water well if the ground is dry in summer and in June, earth up the rows. At this time, top growth should be supported by twine fastened to strong posts at each end of the row. This is necessary to prevent the foliage being broken by strong winds.

In the north lift the tubers before the end of October and keep them in boxes of sand to use as required. In more favourable parts, lift the tubers when needed. The 'Fuseau' variety is the best, smoother and easier to prepare for the table.

Lettuce   Make a sowing in a cold frame or under cloches for an early crop in the north, grow on under cloches or without protection in the south, planting out towards the end of March. The varieties 'All The Year Round' and 'Continuity' are hardy and heart quickly in a well-limed humus-laden soil.

Parsnips   At the month's end, make a sowing of this valuable root crop which requires a long growing season to do well. It is so hardy that the roots may be left in the ground all winter to lift as required. In this way they will best retain their flavour and will not shrivel.

Parsnips require a light friable soil and one that has been manured for a previous crop. A deeply-worked soil is necess-

24

ary for the long roots go down to at least 38cm (15in) deep. Also, be sure to use fresh seed for parsnip seed is difficult to germinate if more than a year old.

Make the drills 38cm (15in) apart and thin the seedlings to 10cm (4in) in the rows, removing alternate plants when they have made some size. Keep the plants watered in dry weather so that they do not become hard and woody as will all roots if they do not receive plenty of moisture. A good variety is 'Tender and True' which makes a thick root, intermediate in length and which is sweet and tender all winter.

If severe weather is expected, lift and store the parsnips in boxes of sand or peat in a shed or garage; or cover the plants with straw in the rows.

Rhubarb Now, or at any time between early November and mid-March when the roots are dormant is the time to lift, divide and plant rhubarb but only when the soil is friable and free of frost.

Lifting is done with a garden fork, inserting it well down so that the long fang-like roots are not broken away. Before lifting, loosen the roots on all sides of the plant. To divide, this is done with a sharp knife or by using two garden forks back to back and prising away the offsets. To grow, each section must have an 'eye' or fruiting bud. This will grow even if part of the root is broken off. But a piece of root without an 'eye' will not fruit. Plant each piece 60cm (2ft) apart in soil enriched with humus and manure such as shoddy or old mushroom compost and with the 'eye' just below soil level. Tread in firmly but take care not to damage the 'eye'. Do not pull any sticks the first year.

This is the time to mulch (top dress) rhubarb before growth begins again. Give the roots a covering of garden compost or decayed manure mixed with peat.

Rhubarb may also be raised from seed sown now or in March. Obtain fresh seed and sow thinly in drills made 2·5cm (1in) deep. Keep moist during spring and summer and in autumn, transplant to permanent beds enriched with humus and manure. Pull no sticks the first season, leaving on the foliage to build up a strong plant.

'Early Albert' or 'Timperley Early' are recommended for

early pulling, or for forcing when three years old. To follow, 'Canada Red' and 'Sutton's Red' produce large crimson sticks of fine flavour whilst 'Victoria' is later.

Shallots At the month's end in the south or early March in the north, plant shallots if the soil is friable. Shallots need a light friable soil containing humus such as old mushroom compost or decayed manure. Bring to a fine tilth and before planting rake in some bonfire ash or give a 30g/sq m (1oz/sq yd) dressing of sulphate of potash. Then tread the soil to firm it and plant the bulbs or sets (as small shallots are called) by pressing them into the surface 23cm (9in) apart in the rows with the same distance between them. Hoe regularly between the rows to suppress annual weeds and if the weather is dry, water cöpiously. Watering with dilute liquid manure will improve the size and quality of the bulbs.

'Giant Red' or 'Dutch Yellow' are reliable and will be ready to lift and dry in August. Store in a frost-free room to use over winter. To hasten ripening in a poor summer, bend over the tops of the bulbs in July.

VEGETABLES TO HARVEST IN FEBRUARY

Land cress Also known as American or Winter cress it is widely distributed across N. Europe and is used as a substitute for watercress.

Seed is sown in June or July in shallow drills made 23cm (9in) apart. Later, the young plants are moved to beds of humus-laden soil where they are planted 23cm (9in) apart and kept moist through summer. Late in August, the first shoots are ready to cut and in order to keep them green through winter, surround a part of the bed with boards and cover with a frame light.

Winter spinach A plant of great hardiness, and from a sowing made the previous July, there will be young leaves to pick early in spring and for at least twelve months. Look over the plants often and use the leaves before they become tough. Hardy varieties are 'Long-standing Round' with dark crinkled leaves and 'Sigmaleaf' which has arrow-shaped leaves of good flavour.

26

3 March

GENERAL CULTIVATIONS

The busiest time of the year in the vegetable garden is from early March until the end of May. By early March, the soil of ground freshly prepared and the surface left rough will have been pulverized by wind, frost and rain so that it may now be raked down to a fine tilth.

Keep the hoe moving between the rows of early sown vegetables and those which have occupied the ground since the previous year, such as broccoli and spring cabbage and make sowings of the new season's crops as soon as the soil is friable and the sun begins to warm the land. This will be early in the month in the south; the month's end in the north. It is also time to 'chit' potatoes.

Early in the month obtain seed potatoes, preferably Scottish or Irish grown and which are certified as being free of pest and disease and put these on a layer of peat with the wide or 'rose' end up and close together, in a seed box or tray or egg box. Place in a sunny window or in a light, airy but frost-free room, and by the month's end they will have begun to sprout at the 'eyes'. This will ensure a heavier crop and also see that they get away to a good start.

VEGETABLES TO SOW OR PLANT OUTDOORS IN MARCH

Asparagus The roots or crowns are planted at this time in a bed near those of other permanent crops such as rhubarb. Asparagus is a maritime plant and requires a well-drained sandy soil containing plenty of decayed manure or garden compost. Make a raised bed and plant in trenches 18–20cm

Cloches

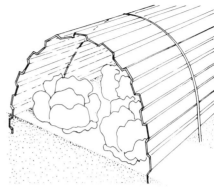

The soil surface beneath a cloche may appear dry but water can flow to the roots of plants as shown

Rigid corrugated clear plastic sheets held in place by wire hoops

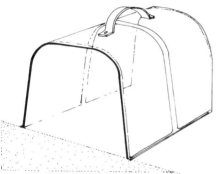

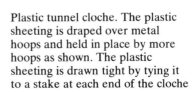

Rigid plastic cloche

Two panes of glass about 30 by 45cm (12 by 18in) forming a tent cloche. The panes can be held by inserting them in a block of wood as shown

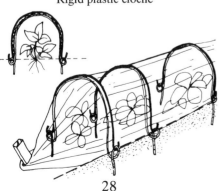

Plastic tunnel cloche. The plastic sheeting is draped over metal hoops and held in place by more hoops as shown. The plastic sheeting is drawn tight by tying it to a stake at each end of the cloche

(7–8in) wide and of similar depth. Place several centimetres of compost in the trench then fill it in with soil to within 8cm (3in) of the top, incorporating 60g (2oz) of superphosphate and 30g (1oz) of sulphate of potash to each metre (yard) of trench. Two to three year old roots will give best results and these are planted over a small mound of soil 90cm (3ft) apart. Fill in the trench and water if dry.

By early May, the shoots will be pushing through the soil but none must be cut the first two years and only one or two from each plant in the third year. Do no cutting after the end of June but allow the remaining sticks to form fern-like foliage which will die back in autumn. Then give a thick mulch.

Using a sharp knife, the sticks are cut from just below soil level and are tied into bundles for cooking, with the tips together.

Reliable varieties are 'Connover's Colossal', with its greenish-white sticks which is the first to mature, and 'Purple Argenteuil' which is later and the favourite of French gastronomes. The sticks are deep purple.

Bean, broad Early in March sow in trenches the 'Windsor' varieties which in colder gardens are not able to survive the winter unprotected. They will be ready late June and extend the season, for those sown in autumn will be ready a month earlier.

Make a trench the width of a spade and incorporate some decayed manure before sowing a double row 18–20cm (7–8in) apart with the beans spaced 15cm (6in) apart in the rows and 5cm (2in) deep. Broad beans like a soil which has been limed for a previous crop. 'Green Windsor' is the best for March sowing.

To discourage black fly, nip out the tops of the plants when about 120cm (4ft) tall. They will then have formed several trusses of pods.

Beet, perpetual Also called spinach beet for although a root crop it is only the leaves that are eaten, cooked like spinach. To make plenty of leaf, it requires a soil containing plenty of nitrogen so work in some decayed manure and rake 30g/m (1oz/yd) of nitrate into the soil on a showery day.

Sow the seed in drills 2·5cm (1in) deep and 45cm (18in) between the rows. The seed is large, like beetroot, and can be spaced 8cm (3in) apart, removing alternate plants as they make growth. Begin using the leaves when they are young and tender as the plants grow quickly.

Broccoli, large-heading Much has been done in recent years to improve the hardiness of broccoli but it should be grown only where a severe winter is not experienced: elsewhere, grow the sprouting broccolis which are easier to manage and hardier. Plants are ready to cut exactly a year from sowing time so that those required for cutting in March are sown the previous March. There are varieties to mature during each of the first six months of the year, depending upon climate and situation.

To withstand the winter, grow the plants 'hard', in a soil manured for a previous crop and which has been given a 30g/sq m (1oz/sq yd) dressing of sulphate of potash or a generous amount of wood ash. Seed is sown in shallow drills in March, April, May and June, the plants being moved to where they are to mature in about a month when they are 8cm (3in) tall. Move on a showery day and plant 60cm (2ft) apart.

One of the hardiest varieties to sow in March is 'Sutton's Safeguard Protecting' which will have formed a large compact head within a year of its sowing. For April sowing, 'Leamington' is reliable and to follow, 'Royal Oak'.

Broccoli, sprouting For colder districts this is, with Brussels sprouts, the most valuable of winter vegetables for the plants are rarely harmed by frost. There are three main types, Early White and Purple sprouting; Late Purple and White sprouting; and perennial White, this being the best form, for if the plants are mulched in summer and kept moist at the roots, they will come again for several years. The Early Purple and White is ready to cut in March (a month earlier in the south-west) one year after sowing whilst the Late Purple and White follow a month or six weeks later. If the weather is mild they mature quickly, forming small cauliflower heads from every leaf joint and it may be necessary to place a quantity in the deep freeze before they run to seed. This is an excellent vegetable to freeze and is especially welcome in winter. The White perennial sprouting comes in May and June, at a time of scarcity of vegetables.

The sprouting broccolis require a soil containing plenty of humus rich in nitrogen when they will make large plants and bear profusely. Plant 90cm (3ft) apart when the seedlings are about 8cm (3in) tall and tread round the plants frequently, otherwise they may be blown over by strong winds.

Brussels sprouts   The most popular winter vegetable, for it begins to form sprouts, like tiny cabbages of almost golf ball size from the leaf joints early in autumn and continues, depending on variety, until late in spring. A dozen plants of two or three varieties will provide a household with a continuous supply.

Sprouts require a soil similar to that provided for the sprouting broccoli, well-enriched with humus and where nitrogen is released over a long period. Hoof and horn meal should be given at a rate of 60g/sq m (2oz/sq yd) and to encourage the plants to produce tightly closed sprouts, rake in at planting time 30g/sq m (1oz/sq yd) of sulphate of potash. Set out the plants 60–90cm (2–3ft) apart and tread in firmly. This will also help to form tight sprouts.

From early October begin to remove the lower sprouts first and keep the plants free of yellowing leaves.

The best early variety, ready by October 1st and productive until the new year, is 'Peer Gynt' which makes a short compact plant and is ideal for a small garden for it can be planted 60cm (2ft) apart. For January–March, 'Citadel' is reliable, being very hardy, and to continue the cropping still later, plant 'Cambridge No. 5'.

Cabbage, autumn   These mature late summer and autumn, bridging the gap between the spring and winter varieties. They mature more quickly than other cabbages; 'Primo' and 'Golden Acre' forming round compact heads within 100 days of sowing. Sow in March and plant out 45cm (18in) apart into soil which was manured for a previous crop. To follow, 'Hurst's Peerless' is useful for November–December cutting.

Cabbage, red This needs a long season to mature. Seed is sown in August in drills, the plants remaining in the rows until mid-March when they are planted 60cm (2ft) apart into well-manured ground. Plant firmly so that they form compact heads and keep the soil moist through summer, and they will be ready to cut for pickling early in autumn, a year after sowing. The new 'Ruby Ball' is the best.

Cabbage, winter These are the monster-heading varieties of great hardiness such as 'Winter White' and 'January King' which needs 9–10 months to mature, when they make large white heads with few outer leaves and are ideal for making coleslaw. They require a soil containing plenty of humus and which releases its nitrogen content over a long period. Sow seed in early March and set out the plants 60cm (2ft) apart. As cabbages do not grow tall, they are suitable for a cold, wind-swept garden.

Calabrese It is the green sprouting or Italian broccoli which if sown in March will be ready late July or early August. This does not grow as tall as other broccolis and first produces a large green head which when removed for cooking will allow numerous shoots to form around the centre stem. It will quickly run to seed in warm weather, so remove the shoots as soon as they form. Plant 45cm (18in) apart in ground which was manured for a previous crop. When cropping has finished, spring cabbage can be planted in its place.

Quickest to mature is 'Express Corona', ready mid-July and which is followed by 'Autumn Spear' which in mild parts will crop until December.

Carrot At the month's end, make a sowing of maincrop carrots in drills, 23cm (9in) apart. Thin the carrots, leaving them about 5cm (2in) apart to grow on to lift in October before the frosts.

Carrots require a soil manured for a previous crop. Fresh manure must be avoided as this causes the roots to 'fork'. Reliable varieties are 'Chantenay Red Cored' and 'Scarlet Perfection' and both freeze well. The almost round 'Parisian Rondo' can be grown in boxes 20cm (8in) deep.·

Sowing carrots out of doors. *Left* a wooden label is used to make a shallow drill. *Right* the seed is placed on a folded sheet of paper, which is gently tapped as it is moved along the drill

Cauliflower To obtain large pure white heads this crop demands care in its culture. It is mostly a summer crop and unless the soil contains plenty of humus, the heads will run to seed when small.

Seed is sown late March and the plants set out 50cm (20in) apart. Plant firmly and if they can be given a mulch when beginning to heart, this will contribute towards their successful culture. But cauliflowers soon lose quality and are better grown in small batches of 20 or so, sowing every three weeks until mid-June.

Early to mature is 'Cambridge Early Allhead' which makes a compact head of excellent texture and this is followed by 'Snow King' which does not easily run to seed in warm weather. For autumn there is 'Early September' and 'Veitch's Self-Protecting', an old and trusted favourite which will stand until Christmas. To preserve the whiteness of the heads, bend over them an inner leaf or two as the curds begin to form. Dust regularly with derris to guard against cabbage white butterflies and their caterpillars.

Kale Also known as borecole and curly kale whilst in olden times it was known as cottager's kale as with its immense hardiness, countrymen could rely on it to provide food in winter. Seed sown in March will produce crinkled fern-like

33

leaves to remove from early September until the end of winter. Plant 45cm (18in) apart in a soil containing some humus to retain summer moisture without which the leaves will be tough and stringy. Begin to remove them whilst still young and tender.

Cottager's kale grows 90cm (3ft) tall but 'Moss Curled' less than 60cm (2ft), its leaves being mild and tender. The new 'Pentland Brigg' is just as hardy.

Kohlrabi Really a cabbage with a swollen stem which forms on top of the soil, and it is this part that is eaten. It has an unusual but pleasant flavour.

To have roots through summer and autumn, make a sowing mid-March and another in early July. Sow in drills 23cm (9in) apart and thin to 13cm (5in) in the rows. A soil manured for a previous crop is suitable. Keep the plants supplied with moisture through summer. The best variety is 'Vienna Green'. Lift the roots when they are tennis ball size.

Lettuce For outdoor lettuce, seed is sown in shallow drills mid-March and every month until early autumn and with frame-grown lettuce will provide an all-year-round crop. Add some humus to the soil and make sure it is well-limed, for in an acid soil, lettuce becomes slimy in wet weather. Sow a small amount of seed often for germination is almost 100%. If you sow too much seed at one time many plants may run to seed before they can be used. Plant the large hearting 'Webb's Wonderful' 38cm (15in) apart and the less robust 'Continuity' which has a bronzy tinge to the leaves but does well in a dry, sandy soil, and 'All The Year Round', 25cm (10in) apart.

Those who enjoy the crisp cos lettuce will find 'Histon Crispie' and 'Buttercrunch' reliable. They are self-folding and heart well. 'Sugar Cos' is also delicious in salads with its sweet flavour.

Onion If seedlings are not raised under glass, plant 'sets'. These are small onions specially prepared and kept at the correct temperature all winter. They are sold by Dutch bulb growers for those gardens which have only a short growing

Purple broccoli stores well in the freezer

Beetroot, a rich well-manured soil is needed to produce a crop like this

season. Sets thus have several months start over seed sown outdoors in March or even under glass.

First break down the soil to a fine tilth and rake in 30g/sq m (1oz/sq yd) of basic slag and 30g (1oz) of sulphate of potash before planting. Then tread the bed and press in the sets 15cm (6in) apart. Keep them well-watered in dry weather and keep the hoe moving between the rows. Late in August bend over the tops to assist ripening, and lift the bulbs early in October before the frosts, and on a dry day, spreading out the onions on sacking to dry off. When dry, rub off the roots and string up in an airy frost-free room to use over winter.

In March sow the spring onion 'White Lisbon' to give salad onions to pull after those sown in autumn have been used. Sow in drills 2·5cm (1in) deep and make another sowing in May. If those sown in autumn are slow to grow, sprinkle a little nitrate of soda between the rows on a showery day.

Savoy   The hardiest of the cabbages, its grooved leaves allow moisture to drain away so that the heads do not decay in wet weather.

The plants require a long growing season and seed is sown in March in shallow drills. Transplant to well-manured ground at the end of April, planting firmly 50cm (20in) apart.

'Savoy King' is reliable and though making a large head, remains tender. To follow, 'Omega' (with its blue-green leaves) will stand until the end of April.

Spinach, summer   This has health-giving qualities and matures quickly. A sowing of round leaf or summer spinach is made in late March and another in May for succession. Ground manured for a previous crop is suitable but some humus to retain moisture in dry weather is important or the plants will run to seed.

Seed is sown in drills 2·5cm (1in) deep and 38cm (15in) apart. If sown thinly there will be no need to thin out the plants. Never allow them to lack moisture. Begin to use the leaves when quite young.

Swede   Known in America as Rutabaga, it is hardier and has better flavour than the turnip and even in cold gardens may be left in the ground all winter, the roots being lifted as required.

Seed is sown in drills 2·5cm (1in) deep at any time between late March and early May. Make the drills 30cm (12in) apart and thin the plants when small to 15cm (6in) apart in the rows.

Turnip Valuable in that the roots mature quickly; from a late March or early April sowing, they will reach tennis ball size in 10–12 weeks, to use until almost the year's end, with the hardier swedes available from January until March.

Sow in drills, in a soil containing plenty of humus, or sow broadcast (like radishes), thinning them when the roots have reached golf ball size, when they are sweet and tender.

For an early crop, 'Tokio Cross' makes a white root and will reach 8cm (3in) in diameter within eight weeks of sowing.

VEGETABLES TO HARVEST IN MARCH

Broccoli, early white and purple sprouting These are hardier and more easily managed than the large-heading varieties and should be in every garden. The early white and purple will be ready early in March and continue until mid-April when the later sprouting varieties begin. They come quickly at this time and the plants need looking over every day, if possible putting the surplus in the freezer for the shoots quickly run to seed in dry and warm weather if left on the plants.

Broccoli, large-heading Varieties such as 'Safeguard Protecting' whose outer leaves fold over to protect the curds (heads) from frost, will be ready to use before the month's end, though the large-heading varieties are best grown south of the Trent when they will continue to grow into good size heads all winter.

Brussels sprouts Those varieties later to mature such as 'Cambridge No. 5' will be productive into March and April. Keep the plants free of yellowing leaves so that the sprouts can receive the maximum of sunlight and moisture.

Cabbage Several of the hardiest winter varieties, almost savoy-like with their crinkled leaves, will stand until March and April. One is 'January King' which has blue-green leaves which fold over to protect the head; another is 'Sentinel' which by March will have formed a head weighing 2·5kg.

Kale   The kales, especially 'Pentland Brigg', will still be bearing succulent curly leaves which make a welcome change from sprouts and cabbages at this time. Cut a few leaves from each plant frequently and use them when young and crisp, and remove all yellowing leaves.

Leeks   Another of those cottager's standbys for they could rely on leeks to survive the severest winter. They will have been available since November. Lift them by placing the garden fork well down beneath the roots so as not to break the stems. Trim off the leaves and roots after lifting.

Savoy   The late maturing 'Omega' will still be available, and into April, when seed is again sown to mature at this time of year. Also reliable is 'Ormskirk Extra Late' which forms a large head of deepest green of excellent flavour.

Seakale beet   Though grown in few gardens this is one of the most delicious and valuable of spring vegetables. The glossy ivory-white stems are removed by pulling at the base as for rhubarb, shortly before required for cooking. Remove the leaves which may be used as a substitute for spinach and cut the stems into 15cm (6in) lengths for stewing. The plants will be productive for many weeks.

The F_1 hybrid 'Vintage Green' is especially tender and rich in vitamins.

Spinach, winter   The variety 'Standwell' with its large succulent leaves and 'Hollandia' which has arrow-shaped leaves will provide plenty of 'green' to use now. A sprinkling of nitrate of soda between the rows at this time will encourage the plants to produce extra leaf. Keep removing the leaves before they grow too large. They have a better flavour when young and this will allow more new leaves to form.

4 April

GENERAL CULTIVATIONS

This is a month of showers and sunshine, a time of vigorous plant growth, and it is desirable to keep a daily look at vegetable plants raised from March sowings and to transplant them to where they are to grow on, before they become too advanced in the drills. Move them with as much soil on the roots as possible, when about 8cm (3in) tall and preferably on a showery day when they will grow away without check. At this time, keep cutting sprouting broccoli which matures quickly and earth up broad beans sown in autumn.

Peas sown earlier will now need staking and there is nothing better than short twiggy sticks for supporting a short variety. These may be collected from woodlands. Insert them between the peas, and around the rows put in a few canes to support twine taken outside the rows about 15cm (6in) above soil level. Fasten another length of twine around the rows at a later date for taller-growing varieties as the plants make growth.

Keep a look out for birds, especially pigeons, attacking young plants, peas especially, and stretch black cotton over the rows about 15cm (6in) above ground; or cover the rows with wire netting pea guards. Birds may also be scared away by fastening tins to canes pressed into the ground at intervals. If held on strings, the tins will 'clink' together in the wind.

April is the time to give spring cabbage and other plants that may have been in the ground over winter, a stimulant such as nitrate of soda or sulphate of ammonia to encourage them to make quick growth. Sprinkle the fertilizer between the rows, no more than 30g/m (1oz/yd), preferably on a showery day.

Early in the month, complete the trenches made during winter for runner beans, leeks and celery. Top up with any remaining compost and add several centimetres of soil in which to plant the seeds or to set out plants.

VEGETABLES TO SOW AND PLANT OUTDOORS

Artichoke, globe It is one of the most handsome of plants and one of the oldest grown by man as food, possibly being introduced into Britain by the Romans from their N. African Empire. It requires a sunny situation but one where it is sheltered from cold winds as it also grows 120–150cm (4–5ft) tall. It must also be remembered that established plants occupy a considerable amount of room.

It is best propagated by suckers which are removed from the parent plant in early April when 15–20cm (6–8in) long. Remove them with a sharp knife with a few roots attached. Plant deeply, 90cm (3ft) apart in rich soil. Work in any form of humus augmented by old mushroom compost, or seaweed for those living at the coast, for like asparagus, this is a maritime plant. At planting time, rake in a 60g/sq m (2oz/sq yd) mixture of kainit and superphosphate of lime. In a well-manured soil, given a mulch each year in autumn, the plants will remain productive for five years but more succulent heads will be obtained if a new bed is made every three years. Keep the plants moist at the roots in summer, and the main heads will grow larger if the lateral heads or shoots are removed when of walnut size. They can be fried whole in butter. Remove the main heads at just the right time. If allowed to remain too long they will be tough. They should be about 10cm (4in) in diameter. Before cooking, remove the pointed tips of the scales. Possibly the green is the best, possessing superior flavour to the purple.

The main heads will be ready towards the end of summer but this can vary with the season. After cutting, cut back the stems to 30cm (12in) above ground, mulch well and earth up the stems. A number of new shoots will arise and if tied together and earthed up again to blanch them, they may, in five to six weeks, be cut and used like cardoons.

Broccoli, large-heading   Those to mature the following April are sown now. Reliable varieties include 'Leamington', 'Knight's Protecting' and 'Lenten Monarch', each forming a large, well protected head of purest white. Sow early in the month and as soon as the seedlings are large enough to handle, transplant to where they will mature.

Cardoon   Closely related to globe artichokes, they are grown in a similar manner, either from suckers removed in April or from seed sown at this time. Sow in drills and when about 8cm (3in) tall move to where they are to grow on, planting them 60cm (2ft) apart each way into a soil containing plenty of humus and decayed manure. They may also be grown in a trench like leeks and celery. Keep well-watered in summer and use the heads before they grow too large, but it is the blanched stems that are more succulent.

Early in October, tie strips of corrugated paper round the stems and earth up (like celery) after removing any yellowing leaves. Blanching will be complete by the month's end when the plants are lifted with soil on the roots. They will store and keep fresh for several months in a frost-free shed or cellar. When cooking, cover in lemon juice or they will turn black.

Good King Henry   A native British perennial, this grows 60cm (2ft) tall and has arrow-shaped leaves. The young stems are used as an alternative to asparagus in May and June, boiled in a little moisture and served with butter. They are first blanched by earthing up in April when they have grown 15cm (6in) long; this they will do in April each year.

Seed is sown early in April in drills made 15cm (6in) apart and as soon as large enough, move the plants to permanent beds containing some humus and decayed manure. Plant 38cm (15in) apart and keep moist during summer. The shoots will be ready to cut the following year and in alternate years, lift and divide half the plants to increase your stock.

Land cress   Also called American cress and Winter cress, it resembles watercress in its dark green leaves and is a valuable supplier of vitamins in a summer or winter salad.

Seed is sown at the beginning of April in a frame or in drills under cloches and at the month's end the young plants will be ready to move to permanent beds enriched with humus and decayed manure. Plant 23cm (9in) apart, keep well-watered and by late summer the first shoots will be ready to cut.

To continue the cropping through winter, surround part of the bed with boards and cover with a frame light. The plants will continue to make leaf through the coldest weather.

Leeks   Those plants raised in a frame will be ready to plant out at the month's end. Take out a trench 23cm (9in) deep and the width of a spade, and at the bottom place some used hops or garden compost and cover this with soil into which is added 30g (1oz) of superphosphate per metre (yard) of trench. If the soil is thrown up on both sides of the trench as it is made, that on one side can be replaced to within 8cm (3in) of the top of the trench whilst that on the other side can be used later for blanching the stems. This begins about September 1st.

To plant leeks, make a hole 15cm (6in) deep with a dibber and drop in a plant, roots first. Do not fill in the hole with soil. This is partly done when watering in after planting. Plant 20cm (8in) apart in the rows, making the rows 15cm (6in) apart. When planting, allow the leaf blade, the broadest part, to fall along the row rather than across it.

Until September 1st, keep the plants supplied with water in dry weather whilst an occasional application of weak liquid manure will increase the size and quality.

Peas   A sowing of a quick-maturing variety is made early in April and also one that will mature later to continue the cropping begun in early summer by those sown in autumn. 'Kelvedon Wonder' and 'Hurst's Beagle' are both wrinkled varieties of exceptional sweetness which grow 45cm (18in) tall and will be ready to harvest by mid-June. To follow, 'Early Onward' is a sport and quick-maturing version of the famous 'Onward', still unsurpassed as a mid-season variety, the pods containing 8 or 10 peas of outstanding flavour whilst 'Recette' is a maincrop variety which bears its pods in threes thus making picking easy whilst it yields enormous crops. A friable soil is necessary, one containing some humus and which has been manured for a previous crop. The ground must not lack lime for of all crops, peas will thrive only in a sweet alkaline soil. Take out a shallow trench the width of a spade and 5cm (2in) deep and make the trench north to south so that all the plants receive their share of sunlight. Sow the seed singly, spacing them 5cm (2in) apart, then fill in with soil to which 30g/m (1oz/yd) of superphosphate has been incorporated. Peas are usually sold in pints and one pint will sow a 6m (20ft) row.

After sowing, it may be advisable to cover the row with wire netting pea guards or black cotton to keep away birds, and as soon as the peas are 2·5cm (1in) above ground, place a few twigs about the rows so that the tendrils may obtain an early hold. Late-maturing varieties such as 'Onward', Recette' and 'Trio' grow to 90cm (3ft) tall and require adequate staking.

Keep the plants well-watered, especially as the pods begin to fill, or the peas will be hard and small and lack sweetness. When harvesting has ended, clip away the haulm and burn it but leave the roots in the ground for they will have converted nitrogen from the atmosphere and have left it in the soil.

Potatoes April 1st is soon enough to plant this valuable food crop and there is much truth in the old adage 'plant early potatoes late and late potatoes early' so begin with the main-crop varieties, but not too soon, so that the shoots do not appear above ground before the month's end or they may be damaged by frost. Remember that the potato is a native of S. America. Situation however does play a big part in deciding when to plant. Growers in Cornwall and S. Wales will be lifting early potatoes before the month's end, when those in the north-east will be planting them. Those gardening south of the Thames may plant in March but elsewhere it is better to wait until the soil is in a friable condition after the winter rains so that there is little chance of the shoots being harmed by late frosts.

Apart from its food value the potato is able to bring 'dirty' neglected land, infested with weeds, into a clean and friable condition whilst the soil will be broken down by regular earthing-up of the haulms. This is the name used for the stems and foliage. Like strawberries, this is one of the few crops that

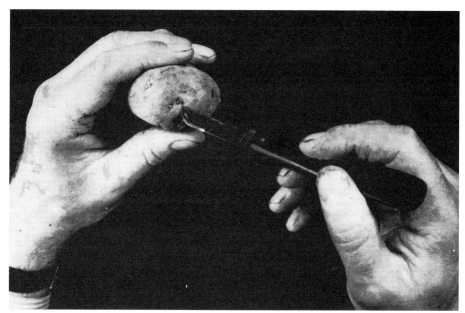

Seed potatoes should have sturdy prominent eyes

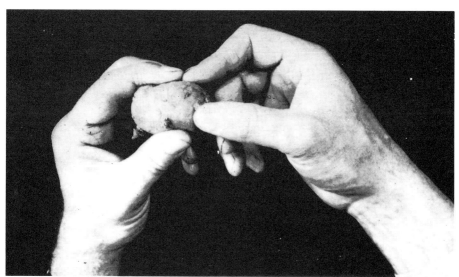

Side shoots should be rubbed out

grows best in a slightly acid soil rather than in one with a high lime content. Potatoes are ideal for peaty soil hence they grow well in the fenlands.

When preparing the ground, give as much peat, bark fibre or old mushroom bed compost as available. If the soil is heavy, work in clearings from ditches and provide material from the garden compost heap to line the trenches, for potatoes are better grown in trenches made 23cm (9in) deep and to a width of a man's size spade. Make the trenches 60cm (2ft) apart to allow for earthing up and align them north to south. An open place is essential as potatoes will not grow in the shade.

When removing tubers from boxes in which they have been 'chitting' (sprouting) take care not to damage the 'sprouts'. If the tubers have not been 'chitted' plant them with their round or 'rose' end uppermost as this is where most 'eyes' will be and it is from the eyes that the sprouts appear. Plant earlies 50cm (20in) apart in rows, allowing slightly more distance for maincrop varieties and press them gently into the compost.

Before filling in the soil which must also be done carefully so as not to damage the 'sprouts', work in 60g/m (2oz/yd) of sulphate of potash and superphosphate of lime. The mixture should be two to one of superphosphate. If the tubers are large, some may be cut into two pieces with the 'eyes' or sprouts as evenly spaced as possible. Rub the cut parts in flowers of sulphur to guard against disease entering. For this reason it is better to use tubers of walnut size rather than to cut them. Cover the tubers with about 10cm (4in) of soil so that the sprouts will not appear above ground until about May 1st when hard frosts should not be experienced. Those gardening in Cornwall and S. Wales may plant towards the end of February and south of the Thames, before the end of March, planting earlies about two weeks later.

For an early crop, 'Arran Pilot' has white kidney-shaped tubers and bears well in all soils whilst 'Home Guard' has round tubers. For a second early 'Sutton's Olympic' with its attractive pink skin is reliable and for maincrop, the long established 'Majestic' and 'Pentland Crown' with its russeted skin are heavy yielders and keep well. Always plant certified seed; these varieties are immune to wart disease.

46

It should be said that where land is low-lying, it is better to plant potatoes on ridges made by earthing up the soil to 15–20cm (6–8in) above the surrounding ground. At the top of the ridge make a V-drill about 10cm (4in) deep and line it with compost before planting the tubers and covering over. The ridges are made 60cm (2ft) apart as for trenches. Earthing-up the haulms and spraying will begin about June 1st when the stalks are 15–20cm (6–8in) above ground.

Radish Make a sowing in early April, either in shallow drills made 15cm (6in) apart or broadcast in beds of well-manured soil as radishes require plenty of humus to hold moisture in dry weather if they are to be successful. They need to grow fast otherwise they will be hard and woody. Make further sowings late in May and early July to give a long succession of roots for the salad bowl.

'French Breakfast', its scarlet roots tipped with white, is most reliable whilst 'Sparkler' makes a round root of similar colour contrast and has flesh that is crisp and sweet. 'Icicle' is all white and makes a tapering root of splendid flavour.

Salsify With its unique flavour this is known as the 'vegetable oyster' and like most vegetables which form a long tap root, it should not be grown in freshly manured soil or the roots will 'fork'. Sow in early April in shallow drills made 30cm (12in) apart, thinning the seedlings to 15cm (6in) apart. Water frequently in dry weather and begin lifting the roots in early November. South of the Trent, the roots may be left in the ground over winter and used as required but those gardening in the north should lift in late November and store in boxes of sand.

Do not peel the roots before cooking as they will 'bleed' and lose flavour. Instead, scrape them and do not omit to add the juice of half a lemon to the water in which the roots are boiled to preserve their whiteness.

'Sandwich Island Mammoth' with roots up to 23cm (9in) long and 2·5cm (1in) thick is the best for flavour.

Seakale About April 1st is a good time to plant seakale thongs which are sent out by nurserymen in bundles. They take more than two years to mature when grown from seed. Thongs are sent out with the top of each cut level, the bottom slanting. They are planted with the level end uppermost about 2·5 cm (1in) below soil level. The soil should contain plenty of humus and as it is a maritime plant requiring salt in its diet, work in 60g/sq m (2oz/sq yd) of kainit when the soil is prepared. Seaweed is also a valuable food for this plant.

It is best to prepare a bed about 150cm (5ft) wide and to plant the thongs 38cm (15in) apart each way. Keep well-watered during summer and in July give a mulch of decayed manure to conserve moisture and suppress weeds.

By mid-October the foliage will die back and should be removed and at the month's end the roots can be lifted, trimmed and stored in damp sand for forcing during winter in a dark place. Small roots or thongs growing around the main roots are removed and stored separately to re-plant next April. 'Lily-white' is the best form, producing long tender shoots of good flavour.

Sugar pea   This has a bean-shaped pod which is sliced like a bean before cooking when it has the tenderness of French beans and the sweetness of peas. Gather in July as soon as the peas can be felt in the pods, when the pods are about 8cm (3in) long for if left too long they will be 'stringy'.

Sow at the end of April in trenches, spacing the peas 5cm (2in) apart as for ordinary peas. Stake in the same way. 'Dwarf Grey' grows 60cm (2ft) tall; 'Burpee's Sweetpod' 120cm (4ft) tall.

Sugar peas require a soil containing plenty of humus to retain moisture in dry weather and a soil that has been limed.

VEGETABLES TO HARVEST IN APRIL
Broccoli, late sprouting   The late white and purple sprouting varieties will begin about mid-April and continue into May. If the weather is warm they will come quickly.

Broccoli, large heading   At this time, 'Leamington', 'Knight's Protecting' and 'Lenten Monarch' will be ready and should be cut when the curds are firm and white. If left too long, they will turn yellow and begin to run to seed.

48

A fine crop of leeks

Cabbage Late cabbages and savoys will still be available, especially 'Ormskirk Late', 'Ice Queen' and savoys 'Omega' and 'Savoy King'. Use them early in the month before the spring cabbages are ready.

Leeks They will be available until the month's end but by then may have become tough and woody.

Lettuce Those plants grown in a frame or set out under cloches early March will be ready to cut at the month's end.

Rhubarb 'Early Albert' and 'Timperley Early' will be ready to pull by mid-April for the first succulent crimson sticks. At this time they are almost the equal of forced rhubarb for tenderness, sweetness and flavour.

Seakale beet This will be ready by mid-April and be at its best until the middle of June. Pull the broad white stems like rhubarb just before required for cooking. The more it is pulled the more it will produce.

Turnips 'Tokio Cross' sown in a frame over a mild hot bed will now be ready, when about 5cm (2in) in diameter. After cooking, they will be sweet and tender.

49

5 May

GENERAL CULTIVATIONS

This is often a dry month after a moist April and the hoe should be kept moving between those plants set out in April. They will now be well-established and for this reason it is advisable to sow most vegetables during March and to transplant in April which is mostly a month of showery weather. Then by early May, the plants will be forming new roots and will take little harm if May and June are dry, which they frequently are.

By mid-May it may be necessary to start watering, for peas and broad beans planted in autumn or early spring will now be forming inside the pods and must not lack moisture at this stage. Also, if they appear to be 'flagging', water newly-planted vegetables. Lettuce also need large amounts of moisture to heart well. It will not be possible to enjoy good crops without the plants being well provided with water.

By the month's end, potatoes will be ready for their first earthing. Take a spade along each side of the rows about 15cm (6in) from the foliage and push the soil right up to the leaves but do not cover them. Earthing will help to conserve moisture and prevent the haulms being broken by strong winds. It will also suppress annual weeds. Jerusalem artichokes and spring-sown Windsor broad beans will also be ready to earth up. They grow tall and earthing will act in the same way as with potatoes. It will also be advisable to fasten a length of garden twine to canes or stakes fixed along the rows to support the foliage.

Sweet corn, aubergines and tomatoes planted at the

month's end or early in June will appreciate some protection from cold winds at this time. A row of twiggy sticks 90–120cm (3–4ft) tall and stuck well into the ground will give useful protection.

Look over the root crops sown in drills in March or early April and thin to 5–8cm (2–3in) apart before they grow too large. In June, remove alternate plants to allow the others more room to develop, using the thinnings in the kitchen.

Make further sowings of mustard and cress (or rape seed) in boxes or frames to use in about three weeks and make regular sowings all the year. Sow more summer spinach at the month's end to crop when that sown March or April is finishing.

VEGETABLES TO SOW OR PLANT OUTDOORS IN MAY

Beans, dwarf Also known as French beans, they are native of N. Africa and in Britain are only half-hardy. In the midlands, seed is sown from May 1st and throughout the month with another sowing early July to continue the cropping through summer. Those gardening in the areas south of the Thames and in the west may sow from mid-April but northern gardeners should delay sowing until the end of May so that the beans will not be above ground until early June when frosts should no longer be present. Where barn cloches are available, sowings can be made a month earlier.

Dwarf beans require a soil containing plenty of humus to hold summer moisture and a little decayed manure. As with all legumes (eg peas and beans) the soil should be friable, well-limed and sweet. An acid soil will never grow good beans.

An open, sunny position is necessary, and the rows should run north to south with 30cm (12in) between each row. Use a trowel to plant the large seeds, putting them 5cm (2in) deep and 15–20cm (6–8in) apart. At the end of a row it is advisable to plant some extra beans to fill in any spaces in the rows where the beans have not germinated. This is an excellent crop for a small garden for the plants grow no more than 25cm (10in) tall and the same amount across, and for the amount of ground they occupy, no plant gives a greater yield. For the first sowing, plant 'Sutton's Premier' or 'The Prince' which mature quickly and will be ready to harvest at the end of June or early July. These varieties are suitable to grow under cloches. In this case, a double row 23cm (9in) apart is sown.

Spray plants under cloches on all warm days, and in the open, from early June. Keep the soil moist, especially as the plants begin to flower and the beans form. The beans will then be succulent and tender. An occasional watering with dilute liquid manure will improve the quality and flavour. French beans must be grown quickly and removed from the plant when about 10cm (4in) long. If left too long on the plant they will be hard and stringy.

To follow 'Premier' and 'Prince', the older 'Masterpiece' is still outstanding in its cropping and for quality. 'Duplex', which bears long stringless pods and 'Gitana', one of the best for freezing, are also reliable.

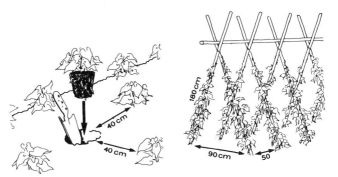

Left Dwarf beans started in pots should be planted out in the open 40cm (16in) apart
Right Diagram of runner bean poles showing traditional method of arranging them

Beans, runner Like the dwarf bean, only half-hardy, it is one of the best of all vegetables, yielding heavily, freezing perfectly and is troubled by few pests and diseases. Growing tall, picking is made easy. It may be grown alongside a path or at the back of the vegetable plot provided it is in an open, sunny position. Cropping so heavily and growing 2·4–3m (8–10ft) tall at the rate of 30cm (12in) a week, it is demanding in soil

Runner beans require plenty of water at this stage of growth

Cauliflower, variety 'Finney'

and food requirements so that trenching is advisable. As mentioned under General Cultivations for earlier in the year, a trench is made in a suitable part of the garden and through the winter, layers of compost, decayed manure, kitchen waste and old newspapers are placed in it until it is almost filled in, and then it is topped up with several centimetres of soil. In April or early May, put in 2·4–2·7m (8–9ft) tall canes or builders' laths, which are rough for the tendrils to cling to, and tie them to strong galvanized wires stretched along the trench about 90cm (3ft) above ground and again at about 150cm (5ft). The canes (or laths) which should be 23cm (9in) apart, have to carry a considerable weight when the plants have reached the top, especially when the plants are wet, so they must be well supported.

Seed is sown, one each side of a cane, about May 1st in the south; mid-May in the north. It is advisable to sow extra seeds in a box or small bed, to have plants available to fill in any that have failed to germinate in the rows. This is an excellent vegetable for freezing and where a deep freeze is available, put in as long a row as possible so as to have runner beans all winter.

Keep the plants well watered, especially when the beans begin to set and help them to do so by giving the plants frequent syringing at the end of each day. Plants growing up canes should be tied in with raffia when 15cm (6in) tall which will encourage them to twine. Early in July, give the rows a mulch of strawy manure or garden compost. Kidney beans as they are also called from the shape of the seeds, may also be grown in tent style, pressing the base of three or four canes into the soil and fastening the tops together. They may be grown in this way wherever there is space about the vegetable garden or even in a mixed border. Remove a circle of soil 25cm (10in) deep and about 50cm (20in) in diameter and fill in with available compost, topping up with soil. Two beans are planted at the base of each cane (or lath).

Reliable varieties are 'Crusader', 'Streamline' and 'Goliath', each producing beans up to 45cm (18in) long and 2·5cm (1in) wide. 'Enorma' is another fine variety. It has long, slender green pods of excellent quality which are suitable for freezing. They will be crisp when 'snapped' if gathered before the seeds can be seen or felt bulging in the pod.

Another form is 'Hammond's Dwarf' which makes a bush only 45cm (18in) tall and so may be grown under barn cloches, planting the seed in mid-April. Make a trench 20cm (8in) wide and 15cm (6in) deep, and sow the seeds about 25cm (10in) apart. Keep the plants watered and spray the foliage often. Remove the cloches early in June when the plants will have reached the top. Harvest the beans when 20cm (8in) long. The first should be ready mid-July or earlier in the south, almost a month before the tall runners are ready.

Beetroot A maritime plant, it is not completely hardy in Britain so that seed is sown in soil manured for a previous crop, from early May. Sow in drills 2·5cm (1in) deep and 23cm (9in) apart and thin out the young plants when they are about 2·5cm (1in) tall, to 10cm (4in) apart in the rows. Before sowing, dress the ground with 30g/sq m (1oz/sq yd) of common salt, preferably on a showery day.

If pelleted seed is sown (this is specially prepared seed covered with a protective coating which breaks down in contact with moisture in the soil), it can be spaced out and thus does away with the need for thinning. Onion and parsnip seed is also obtainable in pelleted form. If ordinary seed is to be sown, rub it gently between two pieces of sandpaper and this will assist its germination. Keep the soil moist after sowing and during the life of the plants for if lacking moisture, the roots will be hard and woody, and they will run to seed early. A second sowing is made mid-June to give a later crop which may be lifted in early October and stored for winter use. Start using the roots when they are about tennis ball size which they should reach by the beginning of August.

'Detroit Globe' is the best round beet. It cooks to deep crimson and is free of paler 'rings'. 'Spangsbjerg Crimson' is an intermediate variety, between the long and ball-shaped beets and has flesh of fine texture.

Celeriac This turnip-rooted celery is hardier than ordinary celery and plants from a March sowing in a frame or over a hot bed can go out after hardening, towards the end of May. Plant into rich, deeply worked soil containing plenty of humus and in rows 45cm (18in) apart, allowing 25cm (10in) between plants. It is important not to bury the bulbous-like root which should just sit on top of the soil. Water in, and keep the soil moist in dry weather. As the roots swell, pull away the soil around them and remove any lateral shoots growing from the bulb with a sharp knife. Feeding once every 10 days with dilute liquid manure from early July will increase the size and quality. By late October, a well-grown root may weigh 1·4–1·8kg (3–4lb). Lift in early November and store in boxes of sand or peat, though the roots will better retain their quality if used from the ground. Cover with straw to keep the ground free of frost and trim off the roots before cooking. They have a delicious celery flavour. 'Marble Ball' is an excellent variety.

Celtuce A lettuce with the celery flavour, the leaves being used raw in a salad or stewed like spinach, whilst the central heart or stem is grated raw into salads or boiled like celery.

Seed is sown about May 1st in the north, a week or so earlier in the south and at three-week intervals until the end of July to provide a succession until late autumn. Sow in shallow drills made 38cm (15in) apart and thin to 23cm (9in) in the rows. A friable humus-laden soil is necessary and in dry weather keep well watered otherwise the plants will run to seed early. Begin using the outer leaves in salads as soon as they form.

VEGETABLES TO HARVEST IN MAY
Asparagus It will be ready to cut from early to mid-May when the sticks are 15–20cm (6–8in) above ground. Using a sharp knife, cut several from each plant, leaving the thinner shoots to form leaf and die back in autumn. The sticks are cut about 2·5cm (1in) below soil level and are tied in bundles for cooking with the tips at one end. Take care not to break off the succulent tips.

Broccoli, perennial white This and the late white sprouting biennial broccoli will be ready from the beginning of May and will come quickly if the weather is warm, the white shoots, like small cauliflowers, appearing from every leaf joint. Use before it goes to seed. The perennial form will produce more shoots in autumn and the following May if it is given a manure mulch in June.

Cabbage, spring May and June is the time when spring cabbage sown the previous July will be ready to cut. They are the most palatable of all cabbages.

Cauliflower 'Early Snowball' grown in a frame will be ready by the month's end and the curds should be used before running to seed.

Kohlrabi Those from a frame sowing over a hot bed in March will be ready towards the month's end.

Kohlrabi belongs to the brassica family

6 June

GENERAL CULTIVATIONS

The main sowings of roots and other vegetables will now be completed and those 'greens' will have been transplanted late in April and early May to use in winter. All that now remains to be done to complete the main planting programme is to plant out the more tender crops such as tomatoes, aubergines, marrows and cucumbers which is done during the first days of June.

This is a warm, dry month, a difficult time for most food crops unless kept well-watered and mulched, though where the soil has been well-fortified with humus, this will go far to preserve moisture at this time. If rain is sparse, water at least once a day, giving the ground a thorough soaking which will reach down to the roots. The roots should never have to turn up to the surface in search of moisture for if they do, the plants will suffer during dry periods. Also frequently syringe the foliage of beans and peas and this will help the flowers to set.

The best time to water in June is early evening for there will be no fear of frosts and the moisture will not be evaporated too soon by the heat of the sun. In the night-time coolness, the plants will become thoroughly refreshed. Without attention to watering, vegetables will make only stunted growth and will be hard and stringy.

In June, keep the hoe moving between the rows. This is best done about mid-day to allow the sun time to kill off any weeds before evening when the plants are watered. Keeping the soil continually stirred will enable the moisture to reach down to the roots more quickly.

Potatoes should be mounded/earthed up as soon as the tops appear above the soil. This will protect them against a late frost and will prevent the tubers from turning green through exposure to light

Continue to earth up potatoes, Jerusalem artichokes and Brussels sprouts too, if the garden is exposed and give runner beans, perennial broccoli, tomatoes and marrows set out early in June, a mulch.

Keep a sharp look out for pests and diseases at this time and take the necessary steps to eradicate them before serious damage is done. Having raised plants of top quality, they must never be neglected in the belief that they will take care of themselves (see spraying chart at end of book). During June, they need all possible help with weeding, watering and spraying.

At the month's end, give the asparagus bed a thick mulch of decayed compost and cut no more sticks for this year. Allow the foliage to die down gradually.

Make further sowings of a quick-maturing cabbage, cauliflower, lettuce and calabrese. At this time, calabrese may be sown thinly in drills made 30cm (12in) apart and left to mature in the rows rather than be transplanted. In this way, they will not run to seed so quickly in warm weather.

Continue to thin root crops, making what may be a second thinning at the month's end and using the thinnings which will now have reached a fair size, in the kitchen.

Make sure that peas are correctly staked for they will not mature quickly if allowed to trail over the ground. The same may be said for spring sown broad beans (the 'Windsors') which should now have the tops removed to discourage black fly and to hasten maturity of the pods.

60

VEGETABLES TO SOW OR PLANT OUTDOORS IN JUNE

Aubergine   Closely related to the potato and also native of S. America, it is frost-tender in Britain and must not be planted out until mid-June, though south of the Thames, it may go out about June 1st. In the north it should be grown in a green-house or frame. It is, however, more easily grown than imagined and in a sunny position outdoors protected from winds, it will crop well in a warm summer.

The plants require a well-drained soil but one enriched with humus and decayed manure such as garden compost or cow manure. Plant 45cm (18in) apart and keep the soil moist otherwise the skins of the plants will crack. Syringe the plants often as this will help the flowers to set and keep the plants free from red spider. At the month's end, stake the plants. Watering once every 10 days with dilute liquid manure will increase the size and quality of fruit.

The fruits will begin to ripen outdoors about mid-August and continue until late September during which time each plant will have produced about 10 egg-shaped fruits each weighing up to 450g (1lb). 'Early Beauty' grows 60cm (2ft) tall and holds its fruit well above ground whilst the F_1 hybrid variety 'Long Tom' bears 30–40 fruits in a season which are shaped like small cucumbers.

Celery   Early June is the time to plant. As for leeks, the ground needs trenching which is done during winter and spring. Make the trench 23cm (9in) wide and 23cm (9in) deep and in the bottom put whatever humus-forming materials there are available. To grow those large, crisp, well-blanched sticks, the plants must have plenty of moisture in summer.

Do not plant out until hardened off, for celery is frost-tender when young though the sticks are improved by frost in winter. As with Brussels sprouts it gives them an added crisp-ness. If possible, plant on a dull day and dip the roots in wet soil before doing so. If planting ordinary celery which will need blanching, allow 8cm (3in) at the top of the trench for this purpose. Plant 23cm (9in) apart in a double row, stag-gering the plants, and for the more vigorous kinds such as 'Lancashire Prize Red', plant 25–30cm (10–12in) apart in

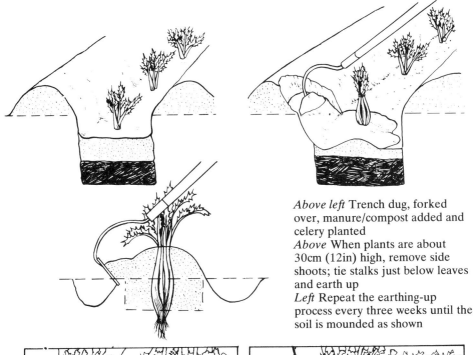

Above left Trench dug, forked over, manure/compost added and celery planted
Above When plants are about 30cm (12in) high, remove side shoots; tie stalks just below leaves and earth up
Left Repeat the earthing-up process every three weeks until the soil is mounded as shown

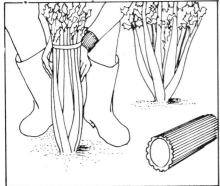

Blanching Celery—Clay Pipes
When the stalks reach about 30cm (12in) high, remove side shoots and tie the stalks together

Fit a clay pipe (or paper collar) around the stalks and gently mound the soil around the base of the clay pipe. Scatter slug pellets

62

rows. Allow 23cm (9in), almost the full width of the trench, between the rows. Blanching begins late in July and you can begin lifting the roots mid-November.

For a small garden 'Cluseed Dwarf White' is recommended for it grows to only half the height of other varieties yet makes a large solid heart. It matures late and is at its best over Christmas.

The self-blanching varieties require no earthing-up and so are set out on the flat but in specially prepared beds, for humus and decayed manure are essential to their growing crisp and succulent. Plant 23cm (9in) apart and water well all summer.

'Golden Self-blanching' is the best to grow, making a large solid heart of palest yellow. But where it is wanted for eating raw or to shred into salads, the sticks will be more tender if lengths of cardboard are fastened round the plants about three weeks before you intend to begin lifting them.

Cucumber, ridge   These are the hardiest varieties, but even so must not be planted out before June 1st; a week later in the north where, in an average summer, they will crop well. They require an open, sunny situation but must not be exposed to cold winds. They grow equally well in deep boxes filled with loam and decayed manure placed on a terrace or balcony and allowed to trail over the sides.

Cucumbers and marrows bear both male and female flowers. *Left* female cucumber flower, clearly showing the ovary which will develop into a cucumber. *Right* male flower without ovary; it will fall off the plant along with its stalk when it fades. Most varieties bear flowers of both sexes on the same plant. However, cucumber varieties bearing only female flowers have been bred

63

Outdoors, plant between ridges, in soil enriched with plenty of humus and some garden compost or decayed manure. The ridges will provide shelter from winds whilst growing between the ridges will mean that the plants receive plenty of moisture during summer. As with marrows, water frequently in dry weather and spray the plants often. At the end of June give the plants a mulch and when they have formed three leaves, stop them to encourage the formation of lateral shoots which will carry the crop. The fruits will begin to ripen late in July and should be used before they grow too large.

Marrows and courgettes Marrows and squashes can be grown in the open, though in the more exposed parts, will crop better if given frame or cloche protection. Those to be grown outdoors are set out about June 1st after hardening off. When manure was in plentiful supply, marrows were planted on a large mound covered with soil and this retained its moisture through summer. Today, with manure scarce, one must use whatever is available such as garden compost augmented by decayed farmyard manure and planting is best done in ridges. Select an open, sunny position (marrows will not grow well in shade) and plant bush marrows 90cm (3ft) apart and trailing marrows 150cm (5ft) apart. If barn cloches are available to cover the plants for three or four weeks when set out, marrows may be planted out mid-May.

Take care when removing the marrows from the pots that the compost does not fall from the roots for marrows resent root disturbance. For this reason they are always best pot-grown. Plant firmly, after making the hole large enough to take the soil ball and insert a small pot into the soil through which the plants are watered. In this way, more moisture will reach the roots. The fruits of marrows are composed of 50% water and the plants need copious amounts if the fruits are to attain any size and be of good quality. When the plants are 45cm (18in) high, nip out the leader shoots to encourage the formation of side shoots and syringe the plants daily in warm weather.

The fruits will begin to ripen in August and should be removed before they grow too large and coarse. What are known as summer marrows, eg 'Table Dainty', 'Casserta', 'Rotherside Orange' and 'Sutton's Superlative' are used when removed or shortly afterwards whilst the winter marrows will store almost through winter. Amongst these are 'Butternut', 'Golden Delicious', 'Royal Acorn', and 'Boston Pie Pumpkin'. These mature later, in September and later still. These are bush marrows: 'Casserta', 'Gold Nugget', Sutton's Superlative', 'Zucchini' (Courgette). These are of trailing habit: 'Rotherside Orange', 'Table Dainty', 'Banana Orange', 'Butternut', 'Golden Delicious', 'Moore's Cream'.

The courgette or zucchini marrow makes a compact bushy plant and matures through summer, the marrows resembling small cucumbers, in that they are used when 15–18cm (6–7in) long. The 'True French' variety can be planted only 38cm (15in) apart.

Sweetcorn Plant sweetcorn out about the second week in June. The plants require an open, sunny situation but one protected from winds. They also need rich, humus-laden soil, which must not lack lime.

Pollination will play a part in planting distances and 38cm (15in) is correct. The male flowers appear at the top of tassel-like inflorescences whilst the females, which produce the cobs, are borne lower down, the silky tassels catching the pollen as it drops from the males above. It is best to plant in blocks or beds of four rows.

Keep the plants moist at the roots and give a mulch of strawy manure in early July. The plants are supported by fixing stakes or canes at each corner of the bed and fastening to them a length of twine about 38cm (15in) above ground and later, at a further 38cm (15in), taken round the outside of the bed. Or insert a cane to each plant, bearing in mind that they grow 150cm (5ft) tall though 'White Midget' grows only 90cm (3ft) tall and should be grown in windy gardens.

Tomatoes After hardening in frames in May, tomatoes to be grown outdoors are set out during the last days of May in the south and about June 10th north of the Trent. Nothing is gained by planting too soon for in some years, frosts persist until early June.

Left Stem of tomato plant showing side-shoots which should be removed
Right Tomatoes defoliated at the base to assist in the ripening of the lower trusses

The ground will have been made ready by digging in plenty of humus, decayed manure and garden compost, whilst peat is much to the tomatoes' liking. Select a sheltered but sunny position for their planting such as a wall facing south, against which the taller-growing varieties are set out 45cm (18in) apart. Those growing under cloches can be planted anywhere in full sun for 'Sleaford Abundance' and 'The Amateur' grow only 45cm (18in) tall.

Ordinary varieties such as 'Moneymaker' and 'Histon Early' which grow 150–180cm (5–6ft) tall will need supporting by canes or stakes and must be tied in every 10 days so that the plants are not damaged by winds. The dwarf kinds need only a few twiggy sticks to hold the foliage and fruit trusses above the soil. They form bushy plants as wide as they grow tall. Plant bush tomatoes 50cm (20in) apart.

If the soil is kept moist, the plants will make rapid growth and at the month's end give them a mulch. Bush tomatoes must be strawed as soon as the first fruits set so as to protect the plants and the fruit from soil splashing in heavy rain.

The flowers will be pollinated by insects. With tall varieties, keep the side growths removed through summer though this is not necessary for bush tomatoes.

VEGETABLES TO HARVEST IN JUNE

Beans, broad Autumn-sown varieties will be ready from the end of May and crop through June when the spring-sown 'Windsors' begin to crop. The beans are removed from the pods before cooking so they should have attained good size before harvesting. Those at the bottom of the plants will be ready first. Remove with care so as not to loosen the plants. 'The Midget' and 'The Sutton' are the first to mature and grow only 38cm (15in) tall so they are the best for an exposed garden.

After all the beans (pods) have been harvested, pull up the plants and place on the compost heap or cut away at ground level and leave the roots to provide valuable nitrogen for the soil.

Broccoli, sprouting The white perennial type will still be producing its snow-white shoots until the month's end.

Celtuce Plants from an early spring sowing will be ready with their leaves by early June. Later in the month, begin pulling the roots so that the centre heart can be grated in salads or stewed as for celery. It has a similar flavour. Sowing at fortnightly intervals until the end of July will maintain a succession.

Lettuce The larger summer cabbage and cos varieties will be ready before the month's end and have a crispness and flavour all their own. 'Sugar Cos' will also be ready by the end of June.

Pea Autumn and early spring-sown varieties will be ready in June, 'Histon Mini' and 'Feltham First' during the first days and 'Early Onward' before the month's end. Harvest them

Pea, variety 'Kelvedon Climax', can be grown without stakes, is sweet in flavour and dark green in colour

when the pods are well-filled and firm but whilst the pod is of emerald green colouring. If it has begun to turn yellow, the peas will have passed their best and have lost flavour and sweetness. A row should crop for two to three weeks. After this cut away the haulm (leaving in the roots) and burn.

Rhubarb The later varieties such as 'The Sutton', a non-seeding variety, and 'Myatt's Victoria' will be ready with their juicy crimson stems.

Spinach, summer Plants from an early spring sowing will be ready to harvest by mid-June and successional sowings will continue the cropping through summer. As summer spinach soon runs to seed, especially in hot, dry weather, begin using the leaves as soon as they are large enough and keep the plants moist at the roots. 'Cleanleaf', with its rounded leaves held well above the soil will need no washing before cooking. The American variety, 'Tampala', is more like a seakale beet in that it forms long thick stems which may be cooked in the same way.

7 July

GENERAL CULTIVATIONS

The previous month will have seen all the season's plantings completed. July is a time for sowing a number of vegetables to use in autumn and winter; also quick-maturing beans and peas to continue the cropping of these vegetables until autumn.

After a usually dry and warm June when vegetables need all possible help in their growing by mulching and artificial watering, July is often a month of thundery showers when plants respond by accelerated growth. On dry days, keep the hoe moving to break up the surface soil and so that the rains may reach the lower roots. Earth up potatoes again, also Jerusalem artichokes, and dust 'greens' with derris powder to kill caterpillars. Look over tomatoes regularly and tie to canes whilst removing all side shoots.

Water runner beans with lime-water to prevent flower drop which in some years can seriously deplete the crop. Also spray the foliage frequently which will help the flowers to set and will keep the plants fresh.

At the month's end, begin to feed tomatoes, aubergines, marrows and ridge cucumbers with weak liquid manure. This should be done once every 10 days until the middle of September and will increase the yield and quality of the crops. Onions too will respond by improved size and quality from liquid fertilizers.

VEGETABLES TO SOW OR PLANT IN JULY

Bean, dwarf The quick maturing 'Limelight', ready to use

69

within two months of sowing early in July, will provide a continuation of French beans until the end of October. Sow in rows made 25cm (10in) apart, spacing the beans 15cm (6in) apart in the rows which are made north to south. Plant with a trowel and into soil which has been manured for an earlier crop. Keep the plants watered in dry weather.

Cabbage, Chinese Also called Pe-Tsai, it originated in the Far East and possesses heat-resisting qualities. It is like a cos lettuce, and is a dual-purpose vegetable, the raw leaves being used in salads during autumn, or steamed, like cabbage. In a dry summer or in a soil not well supplied with humus, the plants tend to run to seed quickly for which reason seed is best sown early July. Dig in plenty of humus such as garden compost and keep the plants watered in dry weather. It is also better to sow broadcast and to thin the plants to 23cm (9in) apart though at first the spacing can be closer and the young plants used in salads when given a final thinning.

'Michihli' is a variety which makes a large heart with dark green leaves and grows 30cm (12in) tall whilst 'Loose-leaved Choy' has quite a different habit, forming a dozen or more greenish stems like seakale beet, at the end of which are spoon-shaped leaves. Use stems and leaves grated in salads or boiled. The new F_1 hybrid, 'Nagaoka', raised in Japan, is valuable in that in autumn it stands several weeks even if the weather is warm.

Cabbage, spring Late July is the time to sow those cabbages which mature the following spring. They mature at a time when Brussels sprouts have finished and spring-sown vegetables have not yet begun to crop. Sow thinly in shallow drills made 23cm (9in) apart and move to their cropping ground late in August or early September, though south of the Trent, planting can continue until the end of October. In the north it is necessary for the plants to have made some growth before the winter. As these cabbages do not grow large, plant them 38cm (15in) apart. They grow conical, the inner leaves folding over to protect the heart from frost and excess rain. Provide them with a soil containing some humus – old mushroom bed compost is suitable – and at planting time, work in a

70

Broad bean, variety 'Green Windsor'

Courgettes, also known as Zucchini

60g/sq m (2oz/sq yd) dressing of basic slag. Keep the hoe moving between the plants in autumn and if the weather is dry water the plants to keep them growing. September is often a dry month but from October 1st, night dews should provide all the moisture needed. Reliable varieties are 'Unwin's Foremost' with its pointed leaves of dark green; 'Flower of Spring'; and 'Early Offenham' which has uniformity of size and shape. 'April' is a new variety of promise and is ready to use in that month. For a small garden, plant 'Durham Elf' which makes a little plant with pointed leaves and is sweet and tender.

Calabrese   If the F_1 hybrid 'Green Comet' is sown about the first week of July, its emerald-green heads or shoots will be available during autumn. It will mature within 60 days of sowing at this time of year and should be sown thinly in drills made 38cm (15in) apart with no transplanting. Keep the plants watered if the weather is dry.

Carrot   Now one may sow carrots in a sheltered garden in the south late in July and begin to pull the roots the following April. The variety 'Frubund', a carrot of Nantes type is sown in drills made 23cm (9in) apart and in a soil manured for a previous crop. Do no thinning until early March so that the young plants will protect each other. In less favourable parts, cover the rows with cloches early in December to bring the plants through a hard winter.

Endive   A delicious ingredient of late summer salads for it is like a densely curled lettuce with a flavour all its own. But it tends to run to seed in dry weather and is best sown early in July with another sowing made at the month's end or early in August. Like Chinese cabbage it is best sown where it is to mature, scattering the seed broadcast in a soil manured for an earlier crop and thinning to 25cm (10in) apart. If plants can be covered with cloches, make a further sowing mid-August to use October until Christmas.

Most varieties of endive are improved by blanching the hearts. As they reach maturity, tie raffia around the outer leaves at the top but only when the plants are dry or they will become slimy. In two weeks, the centre leaves will have become pale golden yellow and can then be used. 'Batavian White' is crisp and tender after blanching. The variety 'Golda' needs no blanching as it forms a close heart whilst it will stand several degrees of frost unprotected. Endive is rather slow to mature, taking three months from sowing time. Keep well-watered if the weather is dry.

Lettuce   Towards the end of July sow the hardiest variety, 'Arctic King', which will stand through winter in all but the coldest parts of Britain. Sow in drills and transplant to rich soil, 30cm (12in) apart. It makes a large heart and has outer leaves of cabbage-like toughness, but the heart is crisp and tender. The first plants will be ready to use early in October. If frosts are hard, cover with cloches in early December.

Radish, winter   The winter radishes, highly popular in Tudor times, remain neglected by modern gardeners yet make a welcome addition to winter salads. Parkinson, botanist to Charles I, said: 'sow them after mid-summer for if sown earlier they would run to seed'. Sound advice and a sowing is made early in July, in drills 23cm (9in) apart. Thin to 13cm (5in) in the rows for the plants will grow as large as a tennis ball. Keep well-watered and lift the roots about mid-November and store in boxes of sand. Sliced in salads they impart a succulent nutty taste.

'Winter Black' has a jet black skin but the flesh is pure white and delicious. 'China Rose' makes a long cylindrical root 8cm (3in) in diameter and has a rosy-red skin and white flesh. It is tipped white at the base. 'Chinese White' is the sweetest of all radishes and is crisp and juicy all winter. Like 'China Rose' it grows 15cm (6in) long and 8cm (3in) in diameter.

Turnip   The variety 'Tokio Cross' will be ready to use within six weeks of a sowing made mid-July, the first roots being ready when about golf ball size early September and they may be used as required until late in November. At this time, sow broadcast and thinly, in soil manured for an earlier crop. Keep watered in dry weather.

Cabbage, variety 'Primo'

CROPS TO HARVEST IN JULY

Beans, broad The March-sown 'Windsors' will be ready late June and early July. Remove them when the beans have reached a good size and have filled the pods but do not leave them too long on the plants for the pods to turn yellow.

Bean, dwarf Varieties 'Tendergreen', 'Masterpiece' and 'Limelight' sown under cloches in May or outdoors in the south, will be cropping by mid-July. Those sown early June will begin at the end of July. Gather them when 8–10cm (3–4in) long and just before they are required for cooking.

Bean, runner 'Hammond's Dwarf' will be ready by the end of July if sown in May under cloches. Harvest the beans when 10cm (4in) long.

Beetroot   By the month's end, late thinnings of early sown beetroot such as 'Detroit Globe' or 'Ruby Queen' will be ready to use.

Cabbage   Spring-sown varieties such as 'Golden Acre' and 'Primo' which make small ball-shaped heads will be ready to use by the month's end.

Calabrese   Plants from spring-sown seed will be ready to harvest by mid-July. Inspect the plants daily and cut the emerald green heads before they start to flower as at this time of year they move quickly from perfect condition to flower.

Onion   The F_1 hybrid, 'Express Yellow' sown in the previous August will be ready to lift by mid-July or if the weather is wet (as it often is in July) leave them in the ground until August. After lifting, leave out on sacks for several hours to dry off before placing on the floor or bench of attic or shed.

8 August

GENERAL CULTIVATIONS

During this month many crops sown or planted in spring will reach maturity. Outdoor tomatoes will be ripening fast and should be kept well watered to increase the size of fruit; aubergines too, also marrows and ridge and frame cucumbers which will now be forming. Feed each of these crops every 10–12 days with dilute liquid manure to increase the size and quality of the fruits. At the month's end 'stop' (take out the growing tips) outdoor tomatoes so that the top trusses will mature by the end of September.

Shallots will be ready to lift towards the month's end and the tops of large onions should be bent over to encourage the bulbs to ripen. Keep the hoe moving between root crops and 'greens' and water thoroughly if the weather is dry. Brussels sprouts especially need plenty of moisture to form large tight sprouts. Runner beans will now be forming quickly so keep the plants well-watered and spray the foliage and flowers each evening. They will benefit from a mulch of strawy manure or garden compost before the month's end and should continue to crop until the end of October. Earth up leeks and celery, using the soil removed when filling the trench with compost.

Early potatoes can be lifted from the beginning of the month. Lift a root to see how large the tubers are and if they have reached about the size of a hen's egg, lift and use without delay. After lifting burn the haulm.

Late peas will now be ready and when these and early potatoes are harvested, the ground can be prepared for spring cabbage, winter spinach and corn salad.

VEGETABLES TO SOW AND PLANT OUTDOORS IN AUGUST

Cabbage, red   This cabbage which is so appreciated when pickled needs a long growing season and seed is sown in drills 2·5cm (1in) deep and 23cm (9in) apart, during August. In the north, the young plants may remain in the rows during winter, to be planted out in early March where they are to mature. South of the Trent, move them in early October, planting 50cm (20in) apart into soil containing plenty of humus such as garden compost or old mushroom bed manure.

During spring and summer keep the ground moist for the plants need all possible help if they are to make large heads by the following September. In April, give the plants a sprinkling of sulphate of ammonia, preferably on a showery day, to start them into vigorous growth. 'Early Blood Red' is the most reliable variety.

Kohlrabi   So quickly does it mature that if a sowing is made early August in the south (mid-July in the north) in shallow drills made 23cm (9in) apart, the swollen stems, like small turnips, will be ready to use early November. Sow in a soil manured for a previous crop and thin out the seedlings to 15cm (6in) apart. The seedlings will transplant if necessary for it is a cabbage and not a root crop. The new 'Primavera White' is the best variety.

Onion   The new F_1 hybrid, 'Express Yellow' has been specially bred for autumn sowing and is the first large onion to be bred in this way.

Seed is sown mid-August, in drills made 15cm (6in) apart and in a soil manured for a previous crop. Do not move the plants until March when they are planted 15cm (6in) apart into well-manured ground. Keep well watered and take the hoe between the rows often. During May and June give a watering every 10 days with dilute liquid manure and at the end of June bend over the necks to encourage ripening. By mid-July the bulbs will be ready to lift and will be of tennis ball size. They are best used before Christmas.

Rhubarb   Now is the time to plant out rhubarb seedlings sown in spring. A deeply-dug and well-prepared soil is necessary so work in plenty of garden compost and in the north, shoddy or hop manure. Set the plants 45cm (18in) apart each way and tread them in after planting. Keep well watered during autumn and by early November the foliage will die back. The plants will begin to make new growth in March but no sticks should be removed the first year.

Spinach, winter Sow in drills towards the month's end, made 25cm (10in) apart. If sown thinly there will be no need to thin out later. Soil manured for a previous crop will be suitable and keep it comfortably moist until late autumn.

'Long-standing Prickly' is the best variety, the dark green leaves being extensively crinkled to permit excess moisture to drain away. It is hardy and will produce its foliage through winter and spring.

Turnip Sow 'Tokio Cross' early in August and use the roots when of golf ball size during October. Sow in drills 15cm (6in) apart and thin to 8cm (3in) in the rows. Keep the soil moist if the autumn is dry.

VEGETABLES TO HARVEST IN AUGUST

Artichoke, globe It will be ready late in July and during August, but do not allow the globe-like heads to grow too large or they will lose their succulent eating. If the plants have been mulched in June and kept well watered, including an application of liquid manure every 10–12 days until early August, cut the heads when 10cm (4in) across when they will be most tender. Trim off the spines before cooking. If the heads cannot be used all at once remove them with 8–10cm (3–4in) of stem and stand them in water in a cool room. They will remain tender for several weeks but would become tough if left on the plant.

After removing the heads cut down the plants to within 30–38cm (12–15in) of ground level, mulch again and keep well-watered. By late autumn new shoots will have appeared and when about 60cm (2ft) tall, these should be tied together and earthed up. By late October the stems will have been blanched and are then called 'chards'. Cut away and remove the outer skin before cutting into 15cm (6in) lengths.

Above Aubergine, variety 'Long Tom'
Above Left Cucumbers growing in the
greenhouse. Note that good shape is essential
for quality cucumbers, especially for exhibition
purposes
Left Artichoke. The heads should be cut when
10cm (4in) across when they will be most
tender

Cauliflower Varieties sown early such as 'Early Snowball' and 'Snow King' will have formed good sized heads (curds) by early August. They will quickly run to flower at this time.

Garlic In the south, autumn-planted cloves will be ready to lift at the end of August; spring-planted cloves early in October. Lift when the weather is dry and the leaves have turned yellow and store in an open shed to dry off. Then place in string bags in a frost-free room.

Land cress From an early spring sowing, if the plants have been kept growing on, the first shoots will be ready to cut about mid-August and will continue through winter. If hard frosts are normal, cover the plants with cloches about December 1st and in this way the plants will continue to produce their leaves to use in winter salads.

Potatoes Early potatoes will be ready to lift late July in the south-west and during early August elsewhere. Two excellent varieties immune to wart disease are 'Arran Pilot' and 'Pentland Javelin'. Both are very early and heavy croppers, the former producing kidney-shaped tubers, the latter round tubers of creamy white flesh.

Lift with a garden fork which should be pressed well into the ground about 15cm (6in) away from the plant. Sometimes it is better to scrape away the top soil from the plant with a spade until the tubers are exposed so that you may know exactly where they are before using the fork. Remove the haulm and burn it and place the potatoes in boxes and cover with a sack to exclude light. Do not keep the tubers in sunlight or drying wind as they will lose quality. Lift a root or two each day as required to have them at their best.

Shallots If planted early in March in the south, they will be ready to lift at the end of August; in the north about mid-September. Early in August bend over the necks and remove any seed heads to hasten the ripening of the bulbs and lift them at the month's end or when the weather is dry. Spread out on mats or sacking to complete the drying and string up in net bags in an airy but frost-free room to use in winter.

9 September

GENERAL CULTIVATIONS

This is usually a dry, warm month and though the plants will receive moisture from the night dews to keep them fresh, most crops may need watering until the month's end, especially Brussels sprouts, winter cabbages and savoys. Keep the hoe moving between the plants to stir the surface so that moisture will reach the roots and look over the plants each week and remove any yellowing leaves. At the month's end, the first frosts can be expected and it is advisable to bend over a few leaves to protect the heads of cauliflowers and broccoli which are reaching maturity. A hard frost may cause the white curds to turn yellow.

Earth up leeks and celery every fortnight to complete the blanching and look over those tall-growing plants such as Brussels sprouts and sprouting broccoli which will occupy the ground over winter and spring and 'heel in' to make them firm enough to withstand winter winds. Always look over and firm the plants after periods of strong wind. If the garden is exposed, it is useful to earth up all winter 'greens', to give protection against wind and frost.

Partly earth up the swollen base stems or roots of celeriac for this will exclude light and make them more tender when cooked. Before doing so, pull back the soil and remove with a sharp knife any lateral shoots forming on the bulbous part.

As an extra help to leeks in making good size, cut back the leaves at this time to half-way so that the plants will divert available food and moisture into making a long thick stem rather than excess leaf.

As potatoes are lifted and peas and beans gathered, burn the haulms but leave the roots of the legumes in the ground to provide additional nitrogen.

When cabbages and cauliflowers and other crops have been lifted and used, move the unwanted foliage to the compost heap or cut up with a spade and dig in to provide humus for next season's crops. The thick stems should be deeply buried to decay slowly.

VEGETABLES TO SOW AND PLANT IN SEPTEMBER

Bean, broad   Mid-September in the north, October or early November south of the Trent is the time to sow the hardy 'Longpod' broad beans which will survive a cold winter and produce an early crop next summer, before the spring-sown 'Windsors' are ready. In the north, cover the plants with barn cloches by December 1st.

Select a sheltered part for this sowing. Soil manured for an earlier crop will be suitable. Take out a trench 8cm (3in) deep and 23cm (9in) apart and sow with a trowel in a double row made 20cm (8in) apart, allowing 15cm (6in) between the plants in the rows. Plant about 5cm (2in) deep and earth up the plants when they are 8cm (3in) tall. They will not grow much more until early spring.

'Fenland Green' is a hardy longpod and matures early in summer, whilst 'Prolific Longpod' is the best to grow in a heavy clay soil. 'Longfellow' is equally reliable, cropping well in all soils. The long straight pods contain eight or nine beans.

Cabbage, spring   Towards the month's end in the north and during October elsewhere, plant spring cabbage sown in July. Soil manured for a previous crop is suitable as long as it contains plenty of humus. The plants will not grow as large as the winter and summer varieties but have a more pleasant flavour. Plant 38cm (15in) apart as they grow conically, taking up little space. Plant firmly and keep the hoe moving between the rows during dry weather. The plants will continue to grow through winter whenever the weather is mild. Reliable varieties are 'Early Offenham' and 'Flower of Spring'.

Celery inter-cropped with lettuce

Lettuce To mature under glass in early January without heat, sow in September, 'Arctic King' or 'Trocadero'. Sow in drills 15cm (6in) apart and move to a frame in October after clearing it of tomatoes and marrows. Plant 15–20cm (6–8in) apart, dust the plants with a mixture of lime and flowers of sulphur to prevent mildew, and water the soil sparingly. If planting under cloches, plant a double row 20cm (8in) apart in and between the rows. Cover in November with cloches.

For a warm frame, 'Chestnut Early Giant', 'Early Wonder' or 'Kwiek', planted 20×20cm (8×8in) are reliable. 'Loos Tennis Ball' is also reliable, making a golden-green compact head. These specially-bred varieties will heart well in the short days and low light intensity of the British Isles. Others will take twice as long to form a heart.

Onion, spring Early September in the north, late September in the south is the time to sow this popular salad crop for early spring pulling. Sow in shallow drills made 23cm (9in) apart and keep the hoe moving between the rows after germination. Dust the drills with calomel before sowing, to guard against onion fly, and in January dust soot between the rows to absorb winter sunshine and warm the soil. 'White Lisbon' is the best variety to pull 'green' in April and May.

Marrow, variety 'Table Dainty'

Spinach, winter Before the month's end, make another sowing of 'Long-standing Prickly'. A friable soil is necessary so that winter moisture can drain away, whilst soil manured for a previous crop is suitable. Sow thinly in rows made 25cm (10in) apart and thin to 15cm (6in) in the rows. If the garden is exposed, push in some twigs around the rows. North country gardeners will enjoy the crop better if the plants are cloched during the coldest weeks, when protected plants will continue to produce new leaves.

VEGETABLES TO HARVEST IN SEPTEMBER
Beans, runner They will continue until November, if there are no severe frosts.

Beetroot At the month's end or early in October, lift those roots from an early May sowing which have not been used. They will now be the size of an orange but if supplied with moisture all summer, will be tender and sweet.

  Lift with care, especially the long beets for if damaged, the roots will 'bleed' and lose their rich crimson colour. Leave on the fibrous roots and to prevent 'bleeding' screw off the leaves; do not cut them off. Place the roots in an airy room to dry off before placing them in deep boxes on layers of dry peat.

Brussels sprouts   At the month's end (though they are improved by some frost), the early-maturing varieties will be ready. Those sprouts lower down the stem will mature first and they are removed when of golf ball size. Pull them away and at the same time remove any yellowing leaves. As the lower sprouts are removed those higher up the stem will mature. The early varieties such as 'Peer Gynt' and 'Topscore' should be used between now and Christmas, freezing any surplus. The later maturing sprouts begin at Christmas, with the very late varieties cropping until Easter.

Cabbage, Chinese   Plants from seed sown in July will be ready to use by late September. They will not have formed a heart as ordinary cabbage; remove a few leaves from each plant, like winter spinach, and use them raw in a winter salad. Or cook them like spinach. 'Seiko Pac-Choi' is the first to mature, the dark green leaves being held on slender white ribs. It is followed by 'Nagaoka'. Look over the plants often and remove the leaves before they grow too old.

Calabrese   From a sowing of 'Autumn Spear' in June or July shoots will be ready to cut before the end of September. Plants will mature rapidly at this time and quickly run to flower if not removed when at their best.

Endive   Early September will find those plants that have been tied up with raffia ready to use and they will stand until early November. If some plants are then covered with cloches there will be well-blanched heads to use until Christmas. If straw is placed around the plants before cloching, this will give added protection in case of frost.

Kohlrabi   Those from a late sowing will be ready to lift in September and October.

Marrow, winter   The winter marrows mature later and most are of larger size. When ripe, they have a hard skin which protects them in storage. After removing from the plants, place them on a bench or shelf lined with dry straw and also cover the marrows with straw. They will keep several months.

Sweet corn, variety 'Stowell's Evergreen Hybrid'. A hybrid strain, especially bred and selected to mature in the short, cool summers of north-western Europe. It needs a sunny, sheltered site in light, rich soil to fully ripen the cobs

Sweetcorn Early ripening varieties like 'Extra Early Sweet' will be ready to remove late August or September, depending on the amount of sun received for their ripening. Later varieties will ripen at the month's end.

The cobs are removed when the seeds are firm and juicy yet have not become hard. With this crop timing is all-important and they should be used as soon after removing as possible.

Turnip 'Golden Ball' and 'Tokio Cross' (white) sown in spring and early summer will now be ready to lift, though they can remain in the ground until late November. Until then, use them as required, but unlike swedes, turnips are not improved by frost. They will be of grapefruit size but if grown well and not lacking moisture, will be sweet and juicy.

10 October

GENERAL CULTIVATIONS

Watering will now be discontinued as night dews will provide the plants with all the moisture needed. Hoe between the winter 'greens' and earth up celery and leeks again, to complete their blanching. Cover celeriac and parsnips with straw so that lifting can continue through winter.

By the month's end, late-sown dwarf beans and runners will have finished cropping and the plants should be cut away at soil level (leaving in the roots) and moved to the compost heap. At this time there will be plenty of green for composting so build up the heap carefully, adding pigeon or poultry manure if available, some peat and an occasional covering of soil, not forgetting a sprinkling of the compost-maker. There will soon be a heap of top quality compost to dig in or place in trenches during preparation of the ground for next season's cropping.

Now is the time to clear the frames of summer crops eg cucumbers, tomatoes and aubergines. Dig over the soil, incorporating garden compost or decayed manure and some peat and if the frames are not yet to be re-planted with winter lettuce or cauliflowers, remove the lights to allow frost and fresh air to revitalize the soil. At this time, clean the lights with slightly warm soapy water and replace any glass that is broken. Look over heating equipment so that any faults can now be put right and that all will be in running order by early November when some warmth may be required for frame lettuce.

This is also the time to clean seed boxes for new year

sowings. Scrub wooden boxes with warm water into which a little SterIzal has been added, then place in the open for a month for the boxes to be weathered.

VEGETABLES TO SOW AND PLANT IN OCTOBER

Cabbage, spring   Continue to make further plantings during October and November.

Garlic   Gardeners in the south can make a planting of garlic before the end of October which will be ready to lift and use late July or in August, several months before that planted in spring. An open, sunny position is required and a soil manured for a previous crop. The cloves, as the offsets are called, are separated from the bulbs and planted in drills 5cm (2in) deep. Allow 25cm (10in) between the rows and 15cm (6in) in the rows. The soil should be loose and friable. The plants will require no further attention until March when the hoe should be kept moving between the rows.

Peas   Early October in the north, towards the month's end in the south, sow early peas to harvest in May. Use the round-seeded varieties as these do not hold winter moisture like the wrinkled varieties. They are not as sweet but new varieties are not far behind in this respect. For exposed gardens, plant 'Little Marvel' or 'Histon Mini' which grow only 40cm (16in) tall and may be covered with cloches between December and early March. 'Feltham First' and 'Hurst's Beagle' grow to 45cm (18in) and are reliable everywhere. The latter is part-wrinkled and is tolerant of winter wet and is the sweetest and heaviest-cropping of autumn-sown peas. It does however need a friable well-drained soil and should be given a light dressing of lime before working in some humus. Autumn peas are best planted into soil which was made friable and manured for a previous crop.

To sow, take out a shallow trench 5cm (2in) deep and a spade's width and line it with peat. Then sow the seeds singly, spacing them 5cm (2in) apart. Cover with soil which has been given a sprinkling of superphosphate.

When the plants are about 5cm (2in) high, place twiggy sticks about them to give support and to provide some protection from cold winds. If they are to be covered with cloches, see that the sticks are less than cloche height.

To guard against mice, shake up the peas before sowing in a tin containing red lead and a little paraffin, but wash the hands after sowing and bury the tin. Keep red lead locked away from children. Cover the row with pea guards or place small tins held on canes about the rows to scare away wood pigeons.

VEGETABLES TO HARVEST IN OCTOBER

Artichoke, Jerusalem   Lift late October or early November when the tops, which grow 150cm (5ft) tall, have died down. Remove the foliage and after lifting, store the roots in sand or peat. They may however be lifted to use from October 1st or left until near Christmas to use as required, when any remaining tubers are lifted and stored in boxes of peat.

Cabbage, Chinese   Plants from a July sowing will be ready to use late autumn. 'Chihili', which makes a large heart with folding leaves like those of cos lettuce, is especially hardy and withstands several degrees of frost. Cut it and use in salads like lettuce or steam it.

Cabbage, red   Plants from a sowing made the previous year will be ready from early August depending on situation but early October is a suitable time to cut and shred them for pickling. Others can be left until November but not later or they may lose their crispness.

Cabbage, winter   Varieties such as 'Jupiter' and 'Winter Monarch' sown in spring, will by late October be ready to cut and will retain their firmness until Christmas. If you want, they can be pulled from the ground at any time between now and the year's end and strung up (with their roots) in a cool shed or cellar to use when the weather is severe. They will retain their firmness for two months.

Carrot   Near the month's end, lift those maincrop carrots that have not been used before the frosts, and store in a clamp in cellar or garage. Lift carefully as the roots break easily.

90

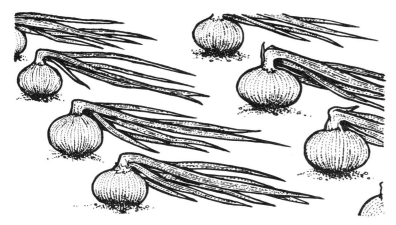

Onions need a long growing season if large, round globes are to be produced. The top-growth has not fallen over: it is bent over to encourage ripening of the globes

Cauliflower The first of the winter varieties will be ready in gardens south of the Humber. 'Sutton's Superlative' and 'South Pacific' will provide large heads at this time whilst for northern gardens, 'Veitch's Autumn Giant' will be at its best in October and November. In the south, it may be used until the year's end when the hardy sprouting broccolis take over.

Onion Those sown in warmth in spring and those grown from sets will have reached 450g (1lb) or more in weight by mid-October and the foliage will have died back. Lift with care so as not to damage the bulbs, and on a dry day, spread them out on sacks to dry off, and before evening move them to an open shed or attic to complete the drying before stringing up in a dry, airy room.

Potatoes Maincrop potatoes will be ready to lift mid-October, before the ground is made wet by November rains. The tubers must be out of the ground and stored before hard frosts. Lift on a dry day and place in paper or hessian sacks after removing as much soil as possible. Place the sacks in a dry, airy and frost-free room such as a cellar or garage and keep them away from light. If possible, cover the sacks with straw or bracken to exclude light and protect from frost.

A clamp may be made at one end of an open shed, garage or cellar. About 120cm (4ft) from the end wall, fix a length of boarding 10–15cm (4–6in) high behind which the potatoes are tipped. Then cover the heap with straw or bracken and place a 5cm (2in) depth of dry soil over it and firm down. For ventilation, it is advisable to insert a short upward-pointing drain pipe at the top of the clamp; or collect some long straws and tie together and insert the bundle in the same way.

Savoy, Tom Thumb Savoy cabbages are round-headed and rather flat-topped; they are easily recognizable by their densely wrinkled leaves. This small and fairly quick-maturing variety may be harvested in early October, perhaps two months sooner than the larger forms.

Seakale By early October, those planted as thongs in March will begin to die back. Remove the foliage now and at the month's end, lift the long roots and after trimming, store in boxes of damp sand in shed or cellar.

From now onwards, provided they can be kept in a dark place, the roots can be forced, in deep boxes in cellar, shed or garage or even in the open, in a seakale 'pit'. This may be constructed against a wall, enclosing an area of 120×120cm (4×4ft) by corrugated sheeting or wooden boards, held in place by strong stakes driven into the ground. Using garden compost or stable manure, a small hot bed is made 30–38cm (12–15in) deep, over which is placed 15cm (6in) of fine soil and peat. Into this, the roots are set 10cm (4in) apart, the crowns level with the top of the soil. A similar hot bed can be made in a shed or cellar, held in place by boards or breeze blocks.

During mid-winter, a temperature of 10–11°C (50–52°F) is necessary to produce tender shoots in reasonable time but a higher temperature will cause the shoots to be tough. In such a temperature and kept moist, the shoots will be ready in about four weeks when they are about eight inches long.

When ready, cut away the shoots just below soil level and just before they are to be used. They may be included raw in a winter salad; or steamed until tender. After cutting the shoots, destroy the roots.

Tomato   These will continue to ripen in a sunny autumn until near the month's end when any left should be picked green to make into chutney. At this time, tomatoes removed when turning yellow will soon turn red (in about three days) if placed on trays in a sunny room or window. After clearing the crop, pull up the plants and burn them.

Tomato, variety 'Alicante'

11 November

GENERAL CULTIVATIONS

By the middle of the month many root crops will have been lifted and stored away from frost, and autumn-maturing 'greens' will have been used to leave a number of bare spaces about the vegetable garden. These may now be made ready for early sowings and plantings next year. Dig over the ground, incorporating whatever humus is available and leave the surface rough to be broken down by frost, wind and rain. If the ground was trenched in January there will be no need to dig deeper than a spit (spade), as long as the humus can be placed about 15cm (6in) below the surface. Give the ground a dusting of hydrated lime to keep it sweet. This is as important as adding humus which will provide the soil with necessary bacteria for healthy plant growth and enable it to retain summer moisture. This is a suitable time to make trenches for runner beans so that they can be filled in with decaying greenstuff, tea leaves and old newspapers during winter.

Do not work the land when in a wet condition or if there is frost in it. Select those days when the soil is in a reasonably friable condition.

Continue to earth up leeks and celery, remove any yellow leaves from rhubarb and winter greens, and firm in broccoli and Brussels sprouts if loosened by winds.

VEGETABLES TO SOW OR PLANT IN NOVEMBER

There are few plantings to be made at this time but for those favourably situated, early peas and longpod broad beans, also spring cabbage, may still be planted if the soil is fairly dry.

94

Plant out winter lettuce and cover with cloches. Cover land cress with cloches for the shoots to continue growing through winter and in exposed gardens, cover autumn-sown peas and broad beans.

VEGETABLES TO HARVEST IN NOVEMBER

Artichoke, globe   The blanched basal shoots left after the globe-shaped heads have been removed, will be ready by November 1st. The shoots when about 60cm (2ft) tall and now called 'chards', will have been tied together before blanching and will resemble a root of celery. After removing, take off the outer skins and cut into 15cm (6in) lengths.

Celeriac   This will be ready to lift from November 1st but will best retain its unique flavour if the roots are left in the ground until required though this may not be advisable in exposed gardens. Hard frost will not harm the roots but the ground may be too hard to lift them when wanted. It will be a help if the plants are covered with straw or bracken about mid-December which is held in place by stones or bricks. This will enable the roots to be lifted in all but the severest weather. If storing in sand or peat, trim off the roots and foliage first. Well-grown roots may weigh 1·3kg (3lb) or more and will be of the size of a large grapefruit. Unlike many roots, it is necessary to peel celeriac before using raw or for cooking as the outer skin is rough and hard.

Celery, self-blanching   This celery will be ready from early October from an early June planting, provided the plants have been well-watered. The sticks may be grated raw into a salad or enjoyed with cheese; or cut into short pieces and boiled to serve with meats and game. It is best to use the outer sticks for boiling and the nutty heart for eating raw.

Though the 'Golden Self-blanching' celery is grown on the flat and without blanching with soil, the outer sticks will be more tender if pieces of cardboard 30cm (12in) wide are tied round the plants a month before using to exclude light.

Chicory   Both the ordinary and winter chicory will be ready to harvest early in November. Plants of the ordinary 'Giant

A heavy crop of self-blanching celery

Witloof' variety raised from an early June sowing will be ready to lift now. The foliage will have died back and the roots will be as thick as a man's wrist. Dig them up with care so as not to break them, trim off any small shoots and they will be ready for forcing.

This is done in cellar or garage and the shoots will be ready in about four weeks, depending on natural warmth at this time or if a little artificial heat is to be used. Or half-fill an orange box with garden compost or old stable manure which still has some warmth in it and cover with 13–15cm (5–6in) of fine soil. Put the roots into this 5cm (2in) apart and water them in. Over the top of the box place sacks or boards to exclude light. There should be 15–20cm (6–8in) between the top of the soil and box top for the shoots to grow. The shoots are broken away with care when 15–20cm (6–8in) long and used raw in winter salads or cooked.

Winter chicory sown in June will now be ready to use in salads. In the south, it can be used until Christmas completely unprotected, but northern gardeners should cover with barn cloches in mid-November and then the plants can be used until almost the end of winter. If no cloches are available, cut the heads, which may weigh 900g (2lb) or more, in early December and place in a drawer in a refrigerator when they will remain fresh for two to three months. The roots are like densely folded cos lettuce but are more tasty and the large inner hearts will be completely blanched.

Kale   Borecole or curly kale is one of the hardiest of winter 'greens' and though early-sown plants can be used from August 1st, it is best left until the frosts when the fern-like fronds will be made crisp and tender. Begin removing a few leaves from each plant during autumn and continue through winter, the younger leaves being more tender than if allowed to grow old.

Parsnip   After a long growing season, plants from a March sowing will have now formed roots which in friable soils, may go down 60cm (2ft) or more though 'Ryder's Intermediate' and 'The Student' will grow less than 30cm (12in). Where there is not a great depth of top soil these varieties should be grown.

Lifting the roots begins early in November and it is no easy task to do so without breaking the ends. First scrape away the soil from the rows and then insert the fork well down along the whole row first on one side, then the other, to loosen the roots partially. Then begin lifting at one end of the row. Store the roots in boxes of sand or leave in the ground if gardening in the south and lift as required through winter for like swedes, parsnips are improved by frost.

Radish, winter   These valuable additions to the winter salad, the black radish and the pink 'China Rose' will be ready to lift early in November. By this time, the black will be of tennis ball size. Lift and trim off the fibrous roots and leaves and place in boxes of peat or sand in a cool room to use as required. They will keep all winter.

12 December

GENERAL CULTIVATIONS

There will be little to do in the vegetable garden at this time unless the winter is mild and the soil in a friable condition when digging can continue, incorporating humus and leaving the surface rough to be broken down by January frosts.

Those roots left in the ground to be lifted as wanted should now be covered with a layer of straw or bracken to exclude hard frost and so make it possible to lift the roots.

Remove any yellowing leaves from the winter 'greens' and if hard frost is expected, fold leaves over the heads of large cauliflowers and broccoli whilst winter cabbage can be removed with soil attached to the roots and placed in a cool room to use when required. Where the garden is exposed, cover peas and broad beans with cloches.

If lettuce and other quick-maturing crops are growing in cold frames, cover the lights with sacking when hard night frost is expected but allow a little ventilation during daytime whenever the weather is mild and sunny.

This is the time to look through the seed catalogues to be ready to place your orders during the first days of January so that seeds for early sowing, especially those plants requiring a long growing season, will be on hand at sowing time. To delay sowing for even a week may greatly reduce the crop. When planning next season's crops, remember to rotate their location, as shown in the diagram.

Inspect and clean all tools, oiling spades and trowels, and clean and tie into bundles canes and laths used for runner beans for they are now expensive to replace and must be treated with care. Put any fertilizers not used into fresh bags or boxes and name them. Store in a dry shed.

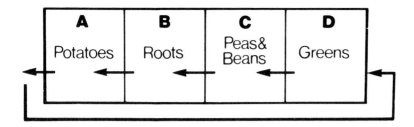

Diagrammatic representation of crop rotation. Crop rotation is most important: if it is not practised serious diseases will build up in the soil and yields will be severely reduced

VEGETABLES TO HARVEST IN DECEMBER

Broccoli, early purple sprouting In the south and west, a mild winter will bring the plants into cropping when the shoots will begin to appear from the leaf joints towards the year's end and may be used when quite small. More shoots will appear if the weather remains mild, and continue until spring when the late sprouting broccolis begin. In the north it will be March before the early sprouting broccolis are ready.

Brussels sprouts Late-maturing varieties will be ready by Christmas but if the early varieties are still productive, use them first and keep the later ones until the new year. Remove any yellow leaves to allow the lower sprouts to develop unhindered and tread in any plants made loose by frost or winds.

Cabbage The large winter varieties such as 'Winter Monarch' and 'January King' will be useful at this time. After the heads have been removed, leave in the stem and roots for these will 'break' into new growth in spring to provide valuable 'greens' at a time of scarcity.

Celery The ordinary varieties which have been blanched will be ready after being made crisp by frost which also brings out the flavour. Pieces of cardboard should have been fastened round the stems before earthing up so as to keep the soil from entering the hearts. By lifting time, the cardboard will have decayed and care must be taken that the soil does not enter the hearts as they will prove difficult to clean if it does. First pull back the soil, then, beginning at one end of the row, insert the fork well down and lift one or more roots as required. If hard frost is expected, place straw or bracken on each side of the row (or double row) which is removed when each plant is lifted. Trim off the roots and remove one or two outer sticks but all the rest can be stewed or eaten raw. There is little waste with celery.

'Ice White' makes sticks 30cm (12in) long and should be used before 'Lancashire Prize Pink' which grows 38–45cm (15–18in) tall and is best kept until the new year.

Leeks So hardy are leeks that they may be left in the ground all winter and it is not necessary to begin using them until late November or December. They can be used until March. By December they will have grown large and thick with the stems blanched for at least 15cm (6in); specialist growers obtain stems of twice this length. Lift with a fork, holding the leaves with one hand and using the fork to prise out the plant with the other hand. Shake off the soil, trim off the basal roots and cut away the surplus foliage but leaving on several centimetres which can be cooked.

Savoy The large-heading varieties with their tightly folding inner leaves which make up and protect the head, will be ready during the coldest months of the year for hard frost will not harm them. If necessary, pull up a few plants and string up in a shed or cellar with the roots on, when they will keep fresh for several weeks. In the open, 'Savoy King' will hold in perfect condition for several months. For later use, 'Omega' will stand until late spring and should be kept until then when greens are scarce.

Swede This is one of the hardiest of roots and may be left in the ground all winter and used as required. Those living in the more exposed parts, where the soil may be frozen for a number of weeks, could cover the rows with straw or bracken mid-December or lift the roots and store in a shed or cellar.

Appendix:
Pests and Diseases

TREATING FOR PESTS AND DISEASES EACH MONTH OF THE YEAR

Month	Plant	Pest or Disease	Treatment
January	Cauliflower Broccoli	Damping Off	Water seed-sowing compost with Chestnut Compound
	All vegetables	Wireworm	Dust soil with Bromophos
February	Tomato	Mosaic	Sow heat-treated seed
	Leek	Eelworm	Sow methyl-bromide-treated seed
March	Carrot	Carrot Fly	Dust soil with Bromophos
	Parsnip	Carrot Fly	Dust soil with Bromophos
	Onion	Onion Fly	Dust rows with calomel before sowing
		White Rot	Treat seed with calomel before sowing as precaution
	Pea	Pre-emergence Wilt	Dust soil with Orthocide at planting
April	Bean, broad	Black Fly	Spray with derris
		Chocolate Spot	Spray with Bordeaux Mixture
	Broccoli Cauliflower Cabbage Savoy	Club Root	Dip roots in calomel before planting
		Root Fly	Treat soil with Lindex
	Carrot	Flea Beetle	Treat soil with Lindex
	Lettuce	Slugs	Treat soil with Slugit solution
		Root Aphis	Treat soil with Lindex when planting

101

Month	Plant	Pest or Disease	Treatment
	Radish ⎫ Swede ⎬ Turnip ⎭	Club Root	Treat rows with calomel before sowing
	Swede ⎫ Turnip ⎭	Turnip Fly	Dust plants with derris and soil with Bromophos before sowing
May	Bean, broad	Black Fly	Dust with derris
	Beetroot	Phoma Lingham	Sow Thiram-treated seed
	Pea	Thrip	Dust plants with Lindex
		Aphis	Dust plants with Lindex
	Turnip		
June	Brussels sprouts ⎫ Cabbage ⎪ Calabrese ⎬ Cauliflower ⎪ Savoy ⎭	Cabbage White Caterpillar	Spray or dust plants with Derris every 2 weeks until end of August
	Celery	Celery Fly	Spray plants with Quassia solution
		Leaf Spot	Spray plants with Bordeaux Mixture
	Cucumber	Leaf Blotch	Spray with Liver of Sulphur Solution
	Pea	Leaf Spot	Spray plants with Bordeaux Mixture
		Aphis	Dust plants with Lindex
	Pepper	Fruit Spot	To prevent, spray with weak Bordeaux Mixture
July	Bean, dwarf	Black Fly	Dust with derris
		Halo Blight	Spray with weak Bordeaux Mixture
	Bean, runner	Black Fly	Dust with Derris
	Artichoke, globe	Leaf Spot	Spray with weak Bordeaux Mixture
	Asparagus	Rust	Spray with weak Bordeaux Mixture
		Beetle	Spray with Derris
	Beetroot	Downy Mildew	Spray with weak Bordeaux Mixture
	Brussels sprouts ⎫ Cabbage ⎪ Spinach ⎬ Lettuce ⎪ Onion ⎭	Downy Mildew	Spray with weak Bordeaux Mixture
	Cucumber ⎫ Marrow ⎭	Powdery Mildew	Spray with Shirlan AG
July	Potato	Blight	Spray with weak Bordeaux Mixture
	Tomato	Blight	Spray with weak Bordeaux Mixture

Month	Plant	Pest or Disease	Treatment
		Botrytis	Spray with Shirlan AG
		Cladosporium	Spray with copper-oil compound
		White Fly	Spray with derris
August	Leek	White Tip	Spray with weak Bordeaux Mixture
	Pepper	Grey Mould	Spray with Shirlan AG
	Aubergine	Botrytis	Spray with Shirlan AG
	Cabbage		
	Brussels sprouts	Cabbage White Caterpillar	Spray with derris
	Broccoli		
	Cauliflower		
September	Mushroom	Phorid & Sciarid Flies	Dust beds with Black Arrow
October	Lettuce (under glass)	Botrytis	Dust with sulphur or Orthocide Captan
	Onion	Smut	Treat soil with Jeyes' Fluid if black spots seen on bulbs
	Potato	Scab ⎫ Wart Disease ⎭	If observed on tubers, in future plant immune varieties
November	Bulbous crops	Eelworm	If observed when lifting, treat soil now with Jeyes' Fluid
December	All vegetables	Wireworm ⎫ Millipedes ⎭	Treat soil when prepared with Bromophos

Index